Planet Cake
CELEBRATE

Cake making for all occasions

Paris Cutler

MURDOCH BOOKS

Contents

....

Introduction

It may come as a surprise that I have devoted this book to cake events rather than just cake decorating. However, for me to write a book it needs to come from my life and at the moment I am spending a lot of time creating, hosting and managing interactive cake events—and I have to admit I am having so much fun!

My ultimate purpose with everything I do is to bring the joy of cake decorating to as many people as possible; however, my goal in this book is to make you look like a rock-star event producer in the process.

This book is for everyone who is hosting an event. There is no need to have knowledge of cake decorating; but even experienced cake decorators will enjoy themselves. I know that these events work because I have created, trialled, tweaked and tested all of them on the harshest critics of all—the general public. I hope to show you that running a successful cake event leaves you feeling like the producer of a sold-out Broadway show and may even earn you a standing ovation.

Imagine you receive an invitation to go to a party where you will meet new people, eat cake, have a laugh, learn how to decorate cupcakes, win a prize, make a social difference via a charity and then finally take your treats home to an audience amazed by your talents. Does this sound like a party you would love to attend? Now you can understand why every event in this book creates a buzz, gets people talking and makes you look like an event guru. It's the power of cake decorating!

One of my most ambitious cake events to date occurred while I was writing this book, when we made the world's biggest Opera House cake—what I call a stunt cake. Weighing nearly 1300 kg (1.3 tons) and taking over a week to make, this cake—and the event—was massive. Think about me as I managed, together with my team, 22 volunteers, logistics, cake technical requirements, lunches, washing up, t-shirts, safety, cake delivery and more. This challenge tested all my cake and event management skills. However, it is a cake event people are still talking about, photos are still popping up on social networking sites, and when it was a success I felt not only that we had achieved something amazing but that I, personally, had the time of my life. What a rush!

I was creating and managing cake events long before I started writing books. Very early in my career I created and hosted my first big cake event—Christmas Charity Cupcake Drive.

My first drive was a huge learning curve in managing mass production and people who had never decorated a cake before. However, we made 1000 cupcakes for the homeless that year and these days the event is so popular that volunteers start registering at the beginning of the year for a spot on the team. We make upward of 5000 Christmas cupcakes for the homeless including dessert for over 2000 Christmas dinners.

In this book I will share with you 10 cake events from small to large. I have kept them simple and you do not need to be a cake decorator to host them. All of the cakes I have designed are for beginners. I have kept the materials and equipment to a bare minimum, you do not need a gourmet kitchen and you do not necessarily need to bake. You just need the instructions in this book, some good organisational skills and enthusiasm. The biggest drawcard for your party will be you, but the cakes make great advertising, and decorating them is an inexpensive and effective party activity.

Be prepared, however, for the 'stayers', the 'lingerers'—guests that tell you your event was a major success by hanging about to decorate just one more cupcake.

I truly believe that the essence of the ongoing food craze is not the good-looking chefs (although they help) or over-the-top cordon bleu cooking—or, in our case, the fact that Planet Cake makes celebrity cakes. It is that the kitchen has historically been the most popular room in the home. The kitchen is usually a warm and safe place, a room where secrets are shared and grief unburdened. Bringing the kitchen into the office, school, hen's night or baby shower—via cake events—will have the same powerful effect of establishing trust and friendship. There is no way you can go wrong with cake, I promise you!

HOW TO USE THIS BOOK

This book has been designed to assist you in planning cupcake and mini-cake events. Each event is based on two designs, so your participants will each create two different designs at your event—other than the School Fete Fundraiser. Each theme is a suggestion only.

The events I have designed and that I regularly run at Planet Cake usually have one of the following goals—to raise money, provide entertainment, highlight a cause and build relationships.

In order to have a fun and successful event, all cupcake designs in this book follow the same principles.

- They are designed for a general audience
- Designs are interchangeable; you can swap or add as your wish
- Preparation times are given for each design, and each takes a short time to assemble
- Equipment and materials are kept to a minimum

Mini cakes are a separate issue and are for a slightly more experienced audience. These events are not designed to be interchangeable with the others. If they are, please note that timing may alter as a result.

GET GOING
Follow these steps:
1 Choose your cake event, activity, competition, fundraising, cause or party
2 Choose your cupcake designs
3 Follow 'How the Party Works' for your chosen event
4 Check the 'Party Planning' section (page 94) for extra planning info
5 Check general information about venue requirements
6 Follow the timeline for your chosen event
7 Photocopy any handouts and templates for guests

Events

Love Sweet Love

Bridal Shower Party

Of all the parties I have organised the most nerve-wracking was a bridal shower for my best friend Melanie, a very stylish modern bride. After my ego overcame the honour of being chosen as 'Hostess with the Mostess', it began to dawn on me just how challenging the organisation of this party was going to be. Guests included a busy bride, bridesmaids, mum, grandma, sister and everyone from future in-laws to Melanie's girlfriends. I had a brainstorm and decided that we needed a theme that involved colour, creativity and connecting with each other. These elements only mean one thing for me—food! Given my experience in our cake decorating school, I knew that a cupcake decorating party would take care of itself if it was well organised. Within 20 minutes of guests arriving I was delighted to see all of Melanie's friends and family mingling together and ganaching cupcakes. Soon I had to turn the music off, as it could not be heard above the raucous sound of women gossiping. As they all had a job to do, the women almost instantly formed a team and the team's focus was Melanie and making her feel cherished. The surprise for me was that the event unfolded even more naturally and successfully than I expected, and we all had the strongest feeling that we were walking along the well-worn path of our grandmothers and great-grandmothers, and indeed of women all over the world. I felt deeply touched by this emotion and I know the other guests did as well.

HOW THE PARTY WORKS

The best way to understand how the party works is to start with the end result. Each guest will leave the Bridal Shower Party with 10 cupcakes (five of each design) that they have proudly decorated themselves, a prize or two, some fun photos, latest gossip and new decorating skills. The cupcake decorating is made up of three parts—ganaching the cupcakes, which is done as a team; covering the cupcakes, which is done as a team; and then decorating the cupcakes, which is usually done individually. There are approximately two days of preparation involved, however this can be performed over a number of weeks and I would recommend enlisting the help of some assistants. It is advisable to have a trial decorating run before the party so that you can give a brief demonstration before each activity. You will also be supported with instruction notes or handouts from this book which you can distribute to guests (see page 100.) The designs I have selected for you are ideal for absolute novices with no cake decorating experience. They look fantastic, however, and are very achievable. If there are poor results it will just add to the hilarity of the event and they may even be suitable for a prize!

See also Party Organiser starting on page 96.

EVENT TIMELINE

- Welcome/aprons on (10 mins)
- Cupcake decorating demo (10 mins)
- Ganaching (20 mins)
- Covering (20 mins)
- Decorating per person (1 hour for 10 cupcakes)
- Photos and prizes (30 mins)
- Box cupcakes and goodbyes

Little Chick Cupcake

EQUIPMENT (per person)

For ganaching and covering cupcakes

Small kitchen knife

Pastry brush

Cranked palette knife

Plastic jug

Small rolling pin

Set of circle cutters

Flexi-smoother

Ziplock bags, to store icing

For decorating cupcakes

Small rolling pin

Set of circle cutters

Small kitchen knife

Fine paintbrush, or frilling tool

Plastic cup

MATERIALS (per person)

5 cupcakes

Syrup (page 109)

100 g (3½ oz) ganache
    (page 108)

200 g (7 oz) yellow fondant
    icing (coverings)

100 g (3½ oz) yellow fondant
    icing (wings)

50 g (1¾ oz) orange fondant
    icing (beaks)

50 g (1¾ oz) black fondant
    icing (eyes)

50 cm (20 inch) white tulle

26-gauge white covered florist's wire

Cornflour (cornstarch), in shaker

> *For colouring fondant icing
>   see pages 122–3.*

1   Ganache and cover the cupcake with yellow fondant icing as per instructions on pages 118–20.

2   Knead the yellow fondant icing for the wings into a smooth pliable dough. Roll out to 3 mm (⅛ inch) thick and using a circle cutter a third of the size of the cupcake, cut a circle. Using the same cutter, trim the circle sides to make two leaf shapes for the wings (Pic a). Using a dab of water, glue the wings to the little chick, tapering the edges with warm fingers.

3   Knead the orange fondant icing for the beak into a smooth pliable dough and roll out to 5 mm (¼ inch) thick. Using a sharp knife, cut out two small diamond shapes. These will become the beak. Use the knife to fold in the middle and dry for a moment on the back of your knife (Pic b). Place on the chick with a dab of water. You can have some fun here using small and large beaks.

4   Using the end of a fine paintbrush (or a frilling tool) indent two holes for the eyes. Roll tiny balls of black fondant icing and stick the balls into the indents.

5   Cut the white tulle for your chicks' veils into 10 cm (4 inch) squares. Using a 1.5 cm (⅝ inch) length of covered florist's wire for each veil, bend it into a hook, loop it through the tulle and twist the ends of the wire together (Pic c).

6   Push the wire ends into the chick's head to attach (Pic d). **Note:** This project is not suitable for children.

a

b

c

d

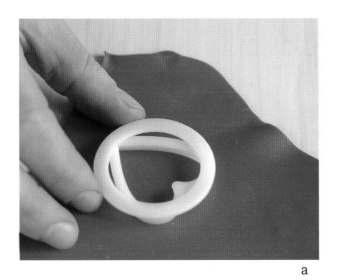

a

b

c

d

Glitter Heart Cupcake

EQUIPMENT *(per person)*
For ganaching and covering cupcakes
Small kitchen knife
Cranked palette knife
Plastic jug
Pastry brush
Small rolling pin
Set of circle cutters
Flexi-smoother

For decorating cupcakes
Small rolling pin
Small and medium heart cutters
Medium paintbrush
Plastic cup
Ziplock bags, to store icing

MATERIALS *(per person)*
5 cupcakes
Syrup (page 109)
100 g (3½ oz) ganache
    (page 108)
200 g (7 oz) white fondant
    icing (coverings)
100 g (3½ oz) red fondant
    icing (medium hearts)
Red edible glitter
50 g (1¾ oz) white fondant icing
    (small hearts)
White edible glitter (optional)
Cornflour (cornstarch), in shaker

> *For colouring fondant icing*
>   *see pages 122–3.*

1 Ganache and cover the cupcake with white fondant icing as per instructions on pages 118–20.

2 Knead the red fondant icing for the medium heart into a smooth pliable dough. Roll out to 3 mm (⅛ inch) thick and, using a medium heart cutter, cut out a heart (Pic a).

3 See glitter technique instructions on page 126. Apply glitter to the red heart and brush off any excess (Pic b). Dab some water on the cupcake and place the red heart on the top. Be careful not to mark the white icing.

4 Knead the white fondant icing for the small heart into a smooth pliable dough. Roll out to 3 mm (⅛ inch) thick and, using a small heart cutter, cut out a heart (Pic c). Dab a very small amount of water on the red heart and place the white heart on top (Pic d).

Optional: Apply white glitter to the small white heart before placing on the cupcake.

Ladies Who Lunch

Birthday Party

This is *a perfect party* for someone like me. I don't really want to make a big deal of my age—okay, so I'm around about 40—and I don't want to drink too much or have an expensive evening. So the idea of spending some time with my girlfriends and making something 'fashionista' at the same time appeals immensely. If it all fails at least we can eat the fudge. The use of fudge for a mini cake is something we have done at Planet Cake for a long time. Fudge is delicious to eat and moulds easily. This event is wonderful to host because there is no preparation, no messy ganache and no cakes to bake. It is simply a matter of gathering the materials and equipment and providing the space. I would suggest that a relaxed approach to this endeavour would be best. Please allow at least two hours for the minis.

HOW THE PARTY WORKS

The best way to understand how the party works is to start with the end result. Each guest will leave the party with two mini cakes (one of each design) that they have proudly decorated themselves, a prize or two, some fun photos, the latest gossip and new decorating skills. The mini-cake decorating is made up of three parts—moulding the fudge, covering the fudge and decorating—all of which are usually done individually. It is advisable to have a trial decorating run before the party so that you can give a brief demonstration before each activity. You can also use instruction notes or handouts from this book that you can distribute to each guest (see page 100). The designs I have selected are for novices with some craft experience. They look fantastic and are very achievable, however they are fiddly. So please remember if there are poor results it will just add to the hilarity of the event—they may even be suitable for a prize!

See also Party Organiser starting on page 96.

EVENT TIMELINE

- Welcome/aprons on (10 mins)
- Mini cake decorating demo (10 mins)
- Mini cake decorating per person (2 hours for two mini cakes)
- Box mini cakes and goodbyes

Mini Handbag Cake

EQUIPMENT (per person)
Small kitchen knife
Pastry brush
Rolling pin
Scissors
Stitching tool
Set of circle cutters
Paintbrush
Tissue
Tweezers

MATERIALS (per person))
100 g (3½ oz) fudge
   (page 106)
80 g (2¾ oz) pink fondant icing
Silver cachous (edible silver balls)
Cornflour (cornstarch),
   in shaker

*For colouring fondant icing
see pages 122–3.*

1 Cut the fudge into a 6 cm (2½ inch) square × 2 cm (1 inch) thick.

2 Cut diagonally through the piece of fudge (Pic a) and then stick the flat sides together, with the narrow ends up, to create the triangular tent shape of the handbag. Brush lightly all over with water.

3 Knead the pink fondant icing into a smooth pliable dough. Roll out to 3 mm (⅛ inch) thick. Cover the fudge bag with the icing. Cut the sides with scissors, trimming excess icing then seal and smooth the edges (Pic b). Mark a centre line down the sides using a small knife.

4 Run a stitching tool over the bag to make a quilting pattern of 1.5 cm (⅝ inch) squares (Pic c).

5 For the flap, roll out pink fondant icing to 3 mm (⅛ inch) thick and use a 6 cm round cutter to cut out a circle of fondant and then cut in half. Stick the half circle to the side of the handbag with a little water (Pic d). Using a stitching tool, make a quilting pattern over the flap (Pic e).

6 For the handle, cut a small strip of fondant icing 2.5 cm (1 inch) long and 5 mm (¼ inch) wide. Attach it to the top of the handbag with a dab of water. Place some tissue under the loop for support and allow to dry. Using tweezers, stick on a silver cachou for the clasp (Pic f).

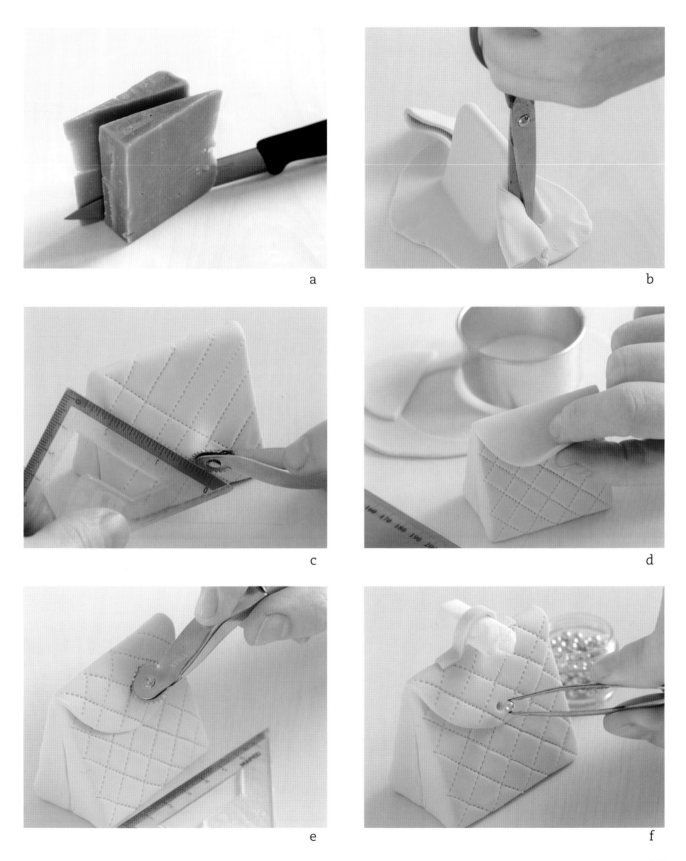

a

b

c

d

e

f

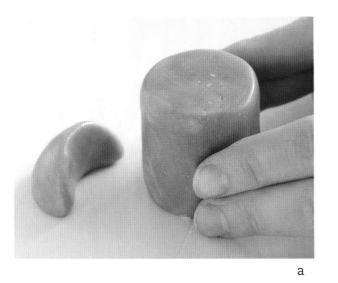

a

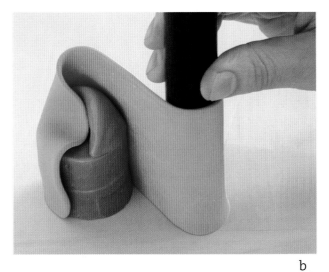

b

c

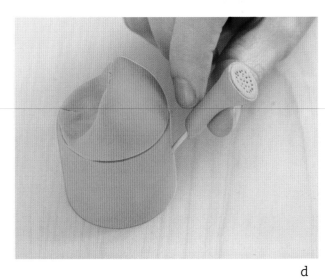

d

e

f

Pink Watering Can

EQUIPMENT (*per person*)
Small rolling pin
Pizza cutter
Small kitchen knife
Medium paintbrush
Pastry brush
Scissors
#2 piping tip

MATERIALS (*per person*)
100 g (3½ oz) fudge (page 106)
5 g (⅛ oz) extra fudge (top of
    watering can)
80 g (2¾ oz) bright pink
    fondant icing
Toothpick or small wooden skewer
10 sugar blossoms (see note)
Cornflour (cornstarch), in shaker

*For colouring fondant icing
see pages 122–3.*

1 Mould the fudge into a cylinder shape. Stand the cylinder upright (Pic a). Mould the extra fudge into a half moon shape and stick it on top of the cylinder. Brush fudge all over with a little water.

2 Knead two-thirds of the bright pink fondant icing into a smooth pliable dough. Roll out to 3 mm (⅛ inch) thick. Cover the watering can with the icing (Pic b). Trim any excess icing and then seal and smooth the edges. Mark rim around the top front of the watering can where the two pieces of fudge meet.

3 Roll some of the remaining bright pink fondant icing into a cylinder that is fatter at one end. Flatten the fat end to form a funnel shape (Pic c). Use a toothpick to mark the holes on the end. Stick a toothpick into the watering can and slide the spout over it to secure it on the watering can (Pic d).

4 Cut a small strip of fondant icing 3 cm (1¼ inch) long and 5 mm (¼ inch) wide. Attach it to the side of the watering can with a dab of water at each end (Pic e). Place some tissue paper under the loop for support and allow to dry.

5 Using a #2 piping tip, mark small studs at each end of the handle. Stick sugar blossoms onto the watering can with a little water (Pic f).

Note: Sugar blossoms are small flowers made from icing. They can be found at most cake decorating shops and some supermarkets. Alternatively, use silk flowers.

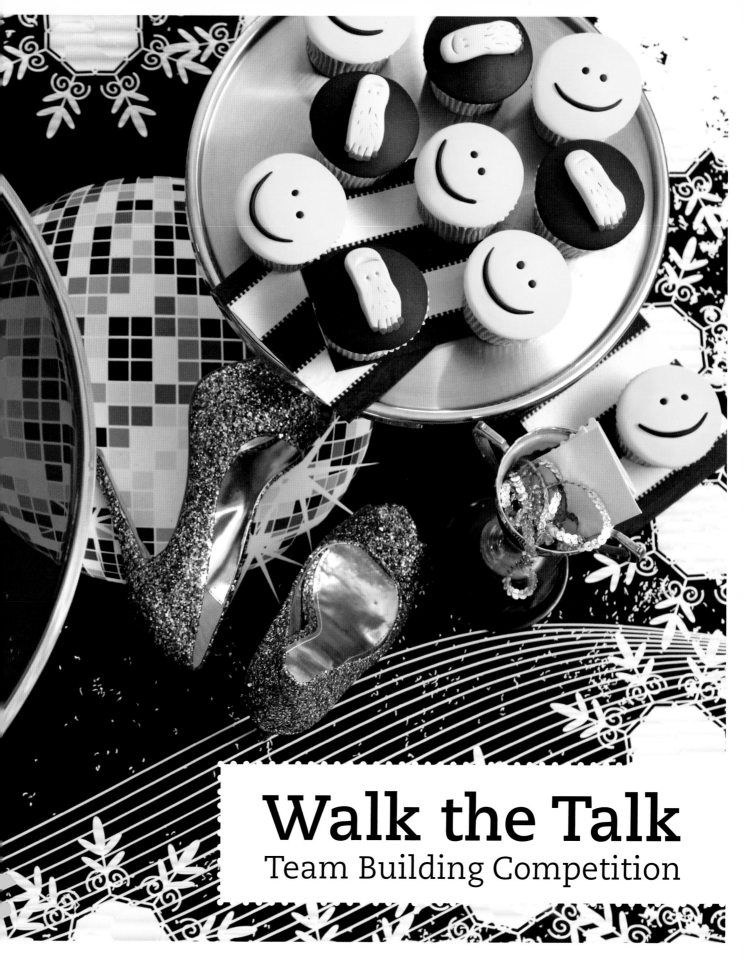

Walk the Talk
Team Building Competition

When we think of a team building activity we automatically think of the corporate world or sports. However, teams exist everywhere—in schools, small businesses, hospitals and even at home. This cake event is incredibly effective because of its simplicity. It gets teams into the kitchen to see who can decorate the best and the most number of cupcakes in the shortest amount of time. In order to win the competition you need to demonstrate all those wonderful attributes that managers wish for—leadership, strategy, time management, effective communication, skill evaluation and teamwork. Everyone must work together to achieve the goal.

I have seen the flexibility of this activity with many companies. You can introduce company logo colours, support a local charity, introduce values and messages, or tailor the event any way you wish. I think the success of this event was summed up for me when a very well-known footballer came to me (all 200 cm of him) and told me it was the best team building event he had been to. He was incredibly proud of his results and was having fun with a team of accountants as though he had known them for years. I am still amazed.

HOW THE EVENT WORKS

This event requires a minimum of 10 people, five people in each team. The goal is for each team member to decorate 10 cupcakes (five of each design) within one hour. For example, a team of five would be required to decorate 50 cupcakes within the hour. They receive a brief 20-minute demonstration on both cupcake designs, including ganaching and covering, then a 10-minute explanation of the competition rules. The teams are shown their cupcakes, ganache and equipment and are expected to proceed for the next hour on their own. They are allowed one lifeline question. The teams that succeed in these events are those that can organise a production line and prioritise their time and resources. This event works best with props (see Extra Pizzazz on page 99).

See also Party Organiser starting on page 96.

COMPETITION RULES

1. Each team has one hour to complete the challenge.
2. Each team member must decorate 10 cupcakes.
3. Each team must decorate an equal number of each design.
4. Extra points are awarded for design improvisation.
5. Extra points are awarded for presentation and neatness.
6. Bonus points are awarded for extra cupcakes decorated.
7. Each team is permitted one lifeline question.

EVENT TIMELINE

- Welcome/aprons on (10 mins)
- Cupcake decorating demo (20 mins)
- Competition rules explained (10 mins)
- Competition per person (1 hour for 10 cupcakes)
- Photos and prizes (20 mins)
- Box cupcakes and goodbyes

Smilie Cupcake

EQUIPMENT *(per person)*

For ganaching and covering cupcakes

Small kitchen knife

Cranked palette knife

Plastic jug

Pastry brush

Rolling pin

Set of circle cutters

Flexi-smoother

For decorating cupcakes

Frilling tool (or small paintbrush)

Set of circle cutters

Medium paintbrush

Plastic cup

Ziplock bags, to store icing

MATERIALS *(per person)*

5 cupcakes

Syrup (page 109)

100 g (3½ oz) ganache
   (page 108)

200 g (7 oz) yellow fondant icing
   (coverings)

100 g (3½ oz) black fondant icing
   (eyes and mouths)

Cornflour (cornstarch), in shaker

> *For colouring fondant icing
>   see pages 122–3.*

1 Ganache and cover the cupcake with yellow fondant icing as per instructions on pages 118–20.

2 Using the end of a paintbrush (or a frilling tool), indent two holes for the eyes (Pic a).

3 Using a medium-sized circle cutter, create an indent for the mouth (Pic b).

4 Roll tiny balls of black fondant icing and stick the balls into the indents.

5 Roll out 5–10 g (⅛–¼ oz) of black fondant icing for the mouth into a very thin sausage. Trim both ends (Pic c).

6 Using a paintbrush, place a thin line of water along the mouth indent and place the sausage for the mouth in the indent (Pic d).

a

b

c

d

a

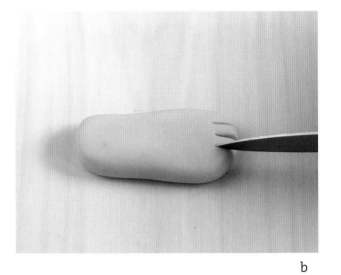

b

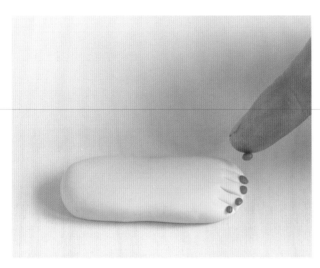

c

d

Hairy Feet Cupcake

EQUIPMENT *(per person)*
For ganaching and covering cupcakes
Small kitchen knife
Cranked palette knife
Plastic jug
Pastry brush
Small rolling pin
Set of circle cutters
Flexi-smoother

For decorating cupcakes
Small rolling pin
Foot template (page 129)
Small sharp knife
Set of circle cutters
Fine paintbrush
Ziplock bags, to store icing

MATERIALS *(per person)*
5 cupcakes
Syrup (page 109)
100 g (3½ oz) ganache
   (page 108)
200 g (7 oz) black fondant
   icing (coverings)
150 g (5½ oz) flesh-coloured
   fondant icing (feet)
25 g (1 oz) red fondant
   icing (toenails)
Black colour paste and cake
   decorating alcohol (hairs)
Cornflour (cornstarch), in shaker

> For colouring fondant icing
>   see pages 122–3.

1 Ganache and cover the cupcake with black fondant icing as per instructions on pages 118–20. See tips on black fondant icing on page 123.

2 Knead the flesh-coloured fondant icing for the foot into a smooth pliable dough and roll out to 4 mm (⅛ inch) thick. Using the template, cut out a foot (Pic a). Smooth the sides of the foot with warm fingers.

3 Using a sharp knife, separate the toes (Pic b).

4 Pinch five tiny pieces of the red fondant icing and roll into balls. Squash each flat to make a toenail shape. Dab the base of the toenails with a little water and stick on the end of the toes (Pic c). Stick the foot in the centre of the cupcake with a dab of water.

5 With the end of a paintbrush, mark two holes for the eyes and use the edge of circle cutter to indent the mouth.

6 To make hairy feet, mix black colour paste with cake decorating alcohol and paint the hairs on the foot using a fine paintbrush as per instructions on page 126 (Pic d).

Baby Garden
Baby Shower Party

Before I fell pregnant with Estelle I really did not understand the baby shower concept. The idea of listening to another round of horror birth stories from well-meaning friends was extremely unappealing. However, luckily for me, my friends threw a surprise shower and not only did I receive a lot of wonderful gifts but I was given something I never counted on—a lot of love. I am now a convert to this precious ritual and I think that this cake event is successful because it is meaningful and appeals to all sexes and ages. It also has a purpose. The idea is to decorate enough cakes for guests to keep some as favours and donate the rest to a children's hospital or women's refuge. Where to distribute your cupcakes is a delightful choice for you to make and depends on the number of cupcakes you have made. You can also make enough for favours only, which is just as much fun. For my best friend's baby shower we had 15 guests, from the elderly to younger people, and of course the mother-to-be. We managed to decorate 100 cupcakes for a local charity. It was wonderful to be able to celebrate the coming of a new baby by giving to other children in our society who desperately need love and care and I felt really proud of the example we set to our children. This event is really about spreading the love, just like ganache on a cupcake—as thick as you like it!

HOW THE PARTY WORKS

The best way of understanding how the party works is to start with the end result. Each guest will leave the Baby Shower Party with up to 10 cupcakes (five of each design) that they have proudly decorated themselves—depending on whether you will be donating any to charity—a prize or two, some fun photos, latest gossip and new decorating skills. The cupcake decorating is made up of three parts—ganaching the cupcakes, which is done as a team; covering the cupcakes, which is done as a team; and then decorating the cupcakes, which is usually done by smaller teams, for example one team per design. Involve children by allocating simple tasks, such as rolling the balls for the caterpillar body. If desired, choose a local charity group.

See also Party Organiser starting on page 96.

EVENT TIMELINE

- Welcome/aprons on (10 mins)
- Cupcake decorating demo (10 mins)
- Ganaching (20 mins)
- Covering (20 mins)
- Decorating per person (1 hour for 10 cupcakes)
- Photos and prizes (30 mins)
- Box cupcakes and goodbyes

Glitter Daisy Cupcake

EQUIPMENT (per person)

For ganaching and covering cupcakes

Small kitchen knife

Cranked palette knife

Plastic jug

Pastry brush

Small rolling pin

Set of circle cutters

Flexi-smoother

For decorating cupcakes

Small rolling pin

Large blossom cutter

Medium paintbrush

Ziplock bags, to store icing

MATERIALS (per person)

5 cupcakes

Syrup (page 109)

100 g (3½ oz) ganache
(page 108)

200 g (7 oz) white fondant
icing (coverings)

150 g (5½ oz) red fondant
icing (flowers)

75 g (2½ oz) red fondant
icing (flower centres)

Red edible glitter

Cornflour (cornstarch),
in shaker

> For colouring fondant icing
> see pages 122–3.

1 Ganache and cover the cupcake with white fondant icing as per instructions on pages 118–20.

2 Knead the red fondant icing for the flower into a smooth pliable dough. Roll out to 3 mm (⅛ inch) thick and, using a large blossom cutter, cut a daisy shape (Pic a). Place the flower on the cupcake with a dab of water.

3 Pinch a ball of the extra red fondant icing the size of a large pea and roll into a ball. Squash flat and sprinkle with red edible glitter (Pic b).

4 Using a soft dry paintbrush, dust off any excess glitter (Pic c).

5 Place in the centre of the flower with a dab of water (Pic d).

a

b

c

d

a

b

c

d

e

f

Baby Caterpillar Cupcake

EQUIPMENT *(per person)*

For ganaching and covering cupcakes

Small kitchen knife

Cranked palette knife

Plastic jug

Pastry brush

Small rolling pin

Set of circle cutters

Flexi-smoother

For decorating cupcakes

Frilling tool

Piping tip

Small kitchen knife

Fine paintbrush

Toothpick or wooden skewer

Drinking straw

Ziplock bags, to store icing

MATERIALS *(per person)*

5 cupcakes

Syrup (page 109)

100 g (3½ oz) ganache
   (page 108)

200 g (7 oz) green fondant
   icing (coverings)

25 g (1 oz) dark brown fondant
   icing (stalk and bite)

150 g (5½ oz) bright pink fondant
   icing (bodies)

25 g (1 oz) white fondant
   icing (hats)

Black colour paste and cake
   decorating alcohol

Cornflour (cornstarch), in shaker

> *For colouring fondant icing
>   see pages 122–3.*

1 Ganache and cover the cupcake with green fondant icing as per instructions on pages 118–20.

2 Using a frilling tool, press a hole into the covering for the apple stalk (Pic a). Pinch a tiny ball of dark brown fondant icing for the stalk and roll into a tiny sausage. Insert in the small hole.

3 Using the blunt end of a piping tip, press an indent for the bite (Pic b). Roll a pea-sized piece of dark brown fondant icing into a ball, then squash flat and press into the indent.

4 Cut nine pieces of bright pink fondant icing for the body, starting from a large pea size down to a baby pea size. Roll each piece into a ball (Pic c). Paint a curved line with water on the cupcake and stick the balls on the cupcake starting from the largest down to the smallest.

5 Pinch a pea-sized piece of white fondant icing for the hat and roll into a small cone (Pic d). Dab the caterpillar's head (largest ball) with water and stick on the cone to make the hat.

6 Mix a little black colour paste with cake decorating alcohol. Use the tip of a toothpick to dot the eyes. Dip the end of a drinking straw into the paste and carefully dab on the mouth (Pics e, f).

Cake Class
School Fete Fundraiser

When I get asked to raise money for a cause, I treat it in the same way as I would my business. The same rules apply to any fundraising event. In order to maximise the financial success of a fete stand you need to have minimal costs and a product or activity that will be irresistible to the general public. The old-fashioned way to make money at a school fete is to bake some cupcakes and sell them. However, parents are time-poor these days and schools require more funding than ever, so getting business-savvy with your cupcakes is a must. Why not get the customers to decorate cupcakes and pay you double for the privilege—and call it a cupcake decorating lesson? In addition, you could hold a public competition for the best cupcakes and encourage some friendly rivalry. I run this type of event several times a year. It does require a minimum team of two cake decorating instructors and a stand manager for crowd control. However, you do not need to be experienced cake decorators. The cupcakes that I have designed for this event are for beginners and have been tested at expos as an interactive cake lesson. All materials are kept to the bare minimum. This event relies heavily on organisation. As soon as people see others at your fete stand decorating cupcakes, they will want to join in. Hang on to your fete stand—you are about to get slammed!

HOW THE EVENT WORKS

When we run these fundraiser cake classes at Planet Cake, we have one instructor per two to three students as well as a stall manager, who books students in for lessons and keeps the logistics flowing. We allow each student to make and take home one design and allow them 10–15 minutes. Time is money so make sure you have some loud timers on hand. Timing will also allow you to calculate how many cupcakes you will require. We set up our stall with 4–6 chairs and a trestle table with the instructors on one side and the students on the other. The cupcakes must be already ganached and the icing colours mixed to save time. This is best done the day before. When the students arrive they are given a step-by-step demo. For example, you might show them how to make the monkey ears and then the students repeat the process. Make sure to set a price for your cupcake lesson—we charge a minimum of $2. When you find yourself fully booked with students waiting, get your store manager to take mobile phone numbers and keep a waiting list so you can call customers when a lesson becomes available.

See also Party Organiser starting on page 96.

EVENT TIMELINE (PER PERSON)

- Welcome student/assess skill base (1 min)
- Recommend design (1 min)—try to keep numbers about even
- Offer latex gloves and/or disposable hand wipes (1 min)
- Cupcake decorating demo (1 min)
- Cupcake decorating per person (10 mins for one cupcake)
- Bag for cupcakes and goodbyes

Cheeky Monkey Cupcake

EQUIPMENT *(per person)*

For ganaching and covering cupcakes

Small kitchen knife

Cranked palette knife

Plastic jug

Pastry brush

Small rolling pin

Set of circle cutters

Flexi-smoother

For decorating cupcakes

Small rolling pin

Monkey face template (page 129)

Small kitchen knife

Frilling tool

Medium paintbrush

Ziplock bags, to store icing

MATERIALS *(per person)*

1 cupcake

Syrup (page 109)

20 g (¾ oz) ganache (page 108)

40 g (1½ oz) brown fondant icing
    (covering)

30 g (1 oz) cream fondant icing (face)

10 g (¼ oz) brown fondant icing,
    extra (ears and nose)

5 g (⅛ oz) cream fondant icing
    (inner ear)

5 g (⅛ oz) black fondant icing (eyes)

Cornflour (cornstarch), in shaker

Red petal dust

For colouring fondant icing
    see pages 122–3.

1 Ganache and cover the cupcake with brown fondant icing as per instructions on pages 118-120. (*This must be done in advance.*)

2 Knead the cream fondant icing for the face into a smooth pliable dough and roll out to 3 mm (⅛ inch) thick. Using the monkey face template and a sharp knife, cut out the monkey face (Pic a). Stick the face on the top of the cupcake with a dab of water.

3 With the frilling tool, mark two holes for the eyes and to indent the mouth (Pic b).

4 Roll a small ball of the remaining brown fondant icing for the ears and flatten slightly. Roll a tiny ball of cream fondant icing for the inner ears and using a dab of water, stick this to the centre of the brown ear and flatten slightly. Cut the circles in half to form two ears.

5 Press the frilling tool into each ball to give them an ear shape. Using a dab of water, stick the ears on the cupcake (Pic c).

6 Roll a small ball of the extra brown fondant icing for the nose and stick in the centre of the face with a dab of water.

7 Roll two tiny balls of black fondant icing and stick the balls into the indents for the eyes.

8 Mix the red petal dust with a little cornflour (to dilute) and dust on each side of the face with a dry paintbrush (Pic d).

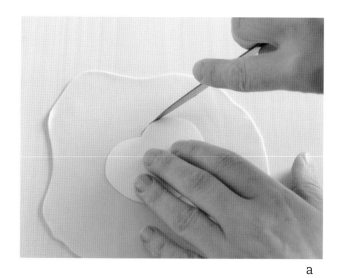

a

b

c

d

Polka Dot Cupcake

EQUIPMENT *(per person)*

For ganaching and covering cupcakes
Small kitchen knife
Cranked palette knife
Plastic jug
Pastry brush
Small rolling pin
Set of circle cutters
Flexi-smoother

For decorating cupcakes
Medium paintbrush
Fine paintbrush
Flexi-smoother
Ziplock bags, to store icing

MATERIALS *(per person)*
1 cupcake
Syrup (page 109)
20 g (¾ oz) ganache (page 108)
40 g (1½ oz) white fondant icing
   (covering)
5 g (⅛ oz) yellow fondant icing (spot)
5 g (⅛ oz) deep pink fondant
   icing (spot)
5 g (⅛ oz) orange fondant icing (spot)
5 g (⅛ oz) purple fondant icing (spot)
5 g (⅛ oz) green fondant icing (spot)
5 g (⅛ oz) aqua fondant icing (spot)
Cornflour (cornstarch), in shaker

> *For colouring fondant icing
> see pages 122–3.*

1 Ganache and cover the cupcake with white fondant icing as per instructions on pages 118-120 (Pic a, b). *(This must be done in advance.)*

3 Pinch off coloured fondant icing for the spots and form into pea-sized pieces. Roll into balls and then squash flat between your fingers to create polka dots (Pic c).

4 Attach polka dots to the top of the cupcake with a very small dab of water.

5 When dry, press gently over the top with a flexi-smoother to smooth them (Pic d).

Lucky Dip
Fudge Cake Fundraiser

I absolutely love this idea for fundraising—my first lucky dip cake event was amazing. I made 100 mini cakes that were all beautifully boxed and bowed. I teamed up with a famous jewellery maker and they offered an incredible prize. One of the mini cakes contained a golden ticket for that prize. However, to win the golden ticket you had to buy a mini cake—and guess how much they were each? Well, let's just say 'very expensive'! The joy in this event rests with its lucky dip appeal; you have to admit that lucky dips are fun. There are many chances to win prizes and if you don't, you still have a gorgeous mini cake. It's fun, it's effective in raising money and, to be quite frank, compared to all the fundraising ideas I have heard of, this one is cool!

HOW THE EVENT WORKS

First, you need to establish how much money you hope to raise from this endeavour—100 mini cakes sold at $100 each is $10 000! Approach a number of businesses for prizes or just one big one. However, if there are many prizes you may be able to raise even more money with your mini cakes. Organise an army of volunteers to help you make the mini cakes and bear in mind that fudge mini cakes can last a while so you can make them over two weeks or so. Making mini cakes requires a patient approach—be careful not to burn out your volunteers. Each cake will take around one hour and I would recommend that each volunteer only makes two per shift. To break that down, if you were to make 100 in one day you would require 15–16 volunteers working solidly for six hours each. In saying this, the end result is worth it and making the cakes is fun in itself. The packaging is most important—see tips on page 97. I would recommend small transparent boxes with the prize details hidden under one of the cakes. This works beautifully when you have all of the cakes on display in their clear boxes. It is a delight to watch participants try to choose the winner.

See also Party Organiser starting on page 96.

CAKE DECORATING TIMELINE

- Welcome/aprons on (10 mins)
- Mini cake decorating demo (10 mins)
- Mini cake decorating per person (2 hours for two mini cakes)
- Photos and prizes (10 mins)
- Boxing and mission begins

High Stakes Present Box

EQUIPMENT *(per person)*
Small kitchen knife
Rolling pin
Pizza cutter
Paintbrush
Pastry brush
Flexi-smoother
Pasta machine (for general use)

MATERIALS *(per person)*
300 g (10½ oz) fudge (page 106)
100 g (3½ oz) white fondant icing
30 g (1 oz) bright pink fondant icing
Cornflour (cornstarch), in shaker

For colouring fondant icing see pages 122–3.

1 Cut the fudge into three pieces, each piece 6 cm (2½ inch) square × 2 cm (1 inch) thick (Pic a). Brush the three pieces with a little water and stack them together to form a cube. Brush the sides of the cube with water.

2 Roll white fondant icing in the pasta machine on #1 setting (Pic b).

3 Cut a strip about 30 × 10 cm (12 × 4 inch). Roll the icing strip around the fudge cube, starting from the middle of one side (Pic c).

4 Using a sharp knife, trim the join (Pics d, e, f). Then smooth the joining line with a warm finger.

5 Cut a square large enough to cover the top of the cube, with overhang down the sides. Place the square on top. Mark sides and cut the lid with a clean knife (Pic g).

6 Roll the bright pink fondant icing in the pasta machine on #4 setting using the fettuccine attachment. Cut the strips into 10 cm (4 inch) lengths.

7 Stick the strips on the cake to form the ribbon around the box, making sure to cover the joining line (Pic h).

8 Roll the leftover bright pink fondant icing to 3 mm (⅛ inch) thick. Cut into two 3 × 5 cm (1¼ × 2 inch) pieces. Fold each piece in half. Pinch over one end of each piece to form the loops of the bow. Place the bow on top of the cake (Pic i).

9 Place a ball of bright pink fondant icing in the middle for the centre of the bow.

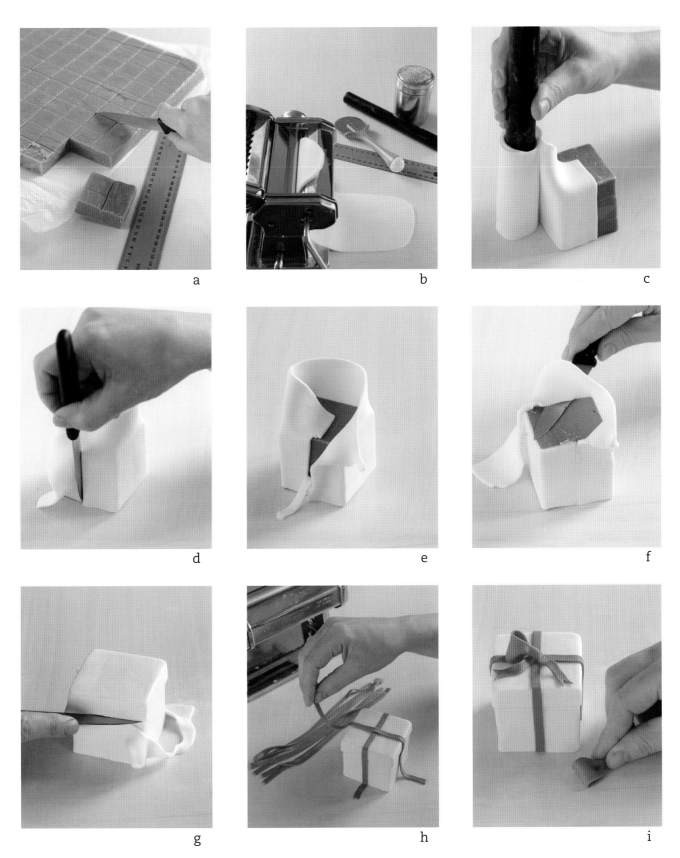

a

b

c

d

e

f

g

h

i

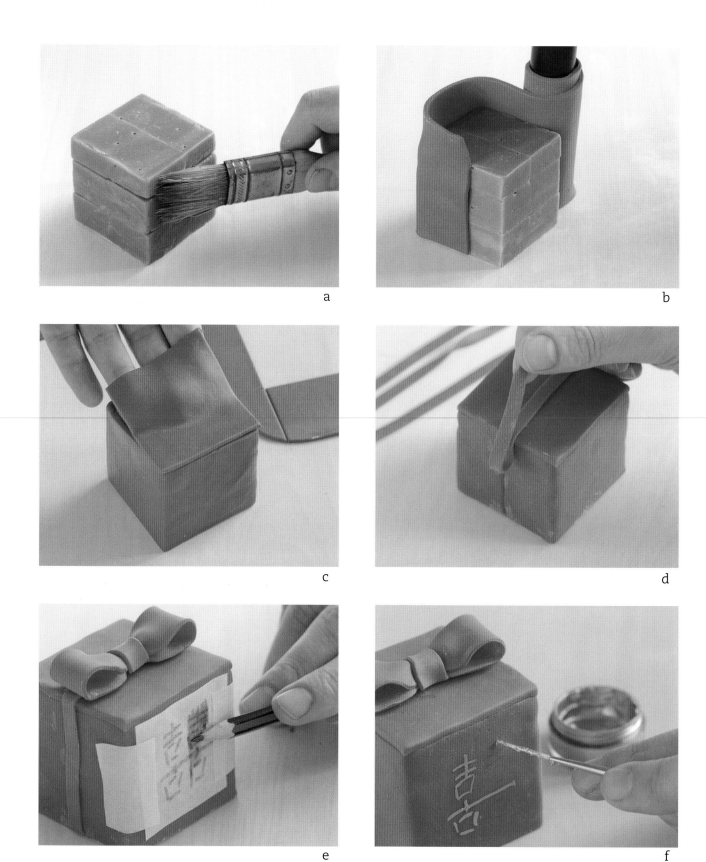

a

b

c

d

e

f

Double Happiness Box

EQUIPMENT *(per person)*
Small kitchen knife
Pastry brush
Rolling pin
Paintbrush
Flexi-smoother
Pasta machine (for general use)

MATERIALS *(per person)*
300 g (10½ oz) fudge
100 g (3½ oz) red fondant icing
50 g (1¾ oz) red fondant icing, extra
Double Happiness template
  (page 129)
Edible gold powder
Cake decorating alcohol
Cornflour (cornstarch), in shaker

> *For colouring fondant icing*
> *see pages 122–3.*

1. Cut the fudge into three pieces, each piece 6 cm (2½ inch) square × 2 cm (1 inch) thick. Brush the three pieces with a little water and stack them together to form a cube. Brush the sides of the cube with water (Pic a).

2. Roll the red fondant icing in the pasta machine on #1 setting as per instructions on page 120. Cut a strip approx 30 × 10 cm (12 × 4 inch).

3. Roll the icing strip around the fudge cube, starting from the middle of one side (Pic b). Trim, then smooth the joining line with a warm finger.

4. Trim the top edge of the icing with a clean knife. Brush the top and edge of the mini cake with water. Roll remaining red fondant icing to 3 mm (⅛ inch) thick. Cut a square large enough to cover the top of the cube. Place the square on top (Pic c).

5. Roll the extra red fondant icing in the pasta machine on #4 setting using the fettuccine attachment. Cut the strips into 20 cm (8 inch) lengths. Stick the strips on the mini cake to form the ribbon, making sure to cover the joining line (Pic d).

6. Roll the leftover red fondant icing to 3 mm (⅛ inch) thick. Cut into two 3 × 5 cm (1¼ × 2 inch) pieces. Fold each piece in half. Pinch over one end of each piece to form the loops of the bow. Place the bow on top of the cake.

7. Using the Double Happiness template, transfer image onto the mini cake as per instructions on page 129 (Pic e).

8. Mix edible gold powder with alcohol. Using a fine paintbrush, paint Double Happiness symbol as per gold painting techniques on page 126 (Pic f).

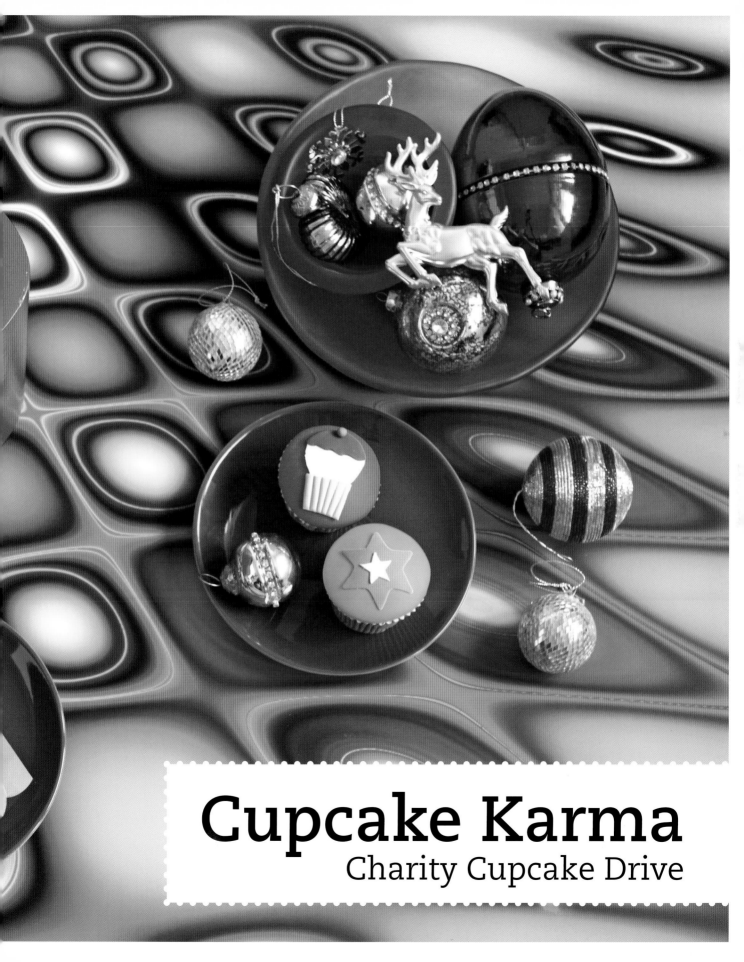

Cupcake Karma
Charity Cupcake Drive

This event is all about decorating as many cupcakes as possible for those in need, either to distribute directly to them, which is what I do with my Christmas Drive, or to sell them to raise money for your chosen cause.

To decorate large numbers of cupcakes you need to form production lines. This is a lot of fun when there is a wonderful goal to be achieved, and beginners and experienced cake decorators can all contribute. This event just requires organisation and energy, but what it gives back is priceless. Without exception, it is always my favourite event of the year. I was inspired to create this event by an incredible woman named Deborah Lee; she has worked tirelessly for children, and has fostered over 100 babies. Something Deborah said hit a nerve. She pointed out that many disadvantaged people are given the staples of existence—food, clothing, etc.—but she marvelled at the positive effect that a perfumed bar of soap or a nice treat could bring to their morale, which was just as important in helping them deal with their current circumstances. Hence I started the cupcake drive. I enlisted the help of a charity food company which agreed to distribute the cupcakes along with their normal run and I gave it a shot. The event was so successful that I had charities contacting me directly, particularly women's refuges asking for cupcakes for the children in their care. Christmas time is usually when charities and shelters are at their busiest and their needs are greatest.

HOW THE EVENT WORKS

You need to set a target for your drive. For my first drive we set a target of 1000 cupcakes, but for novices 250 cupcakes should be ample. Your first challenge will be to get your hands on that many cupcakes. My three suggestions are: ask each volunteer to bake and bring their own, approach your local baker for a donation, or charge your volunteers an entry fee to cover the cost of materials (for example, $10 each). Once you have set your target and your times, and hence the numbers of volunteers required, enlist your army of volunteers. Set decorating shifts of two hours as it is too much to expect beginners to be decorating for hours on end. In one hour you can estimate that each volunteer should be able to decorate about 10 cupcakes (five of each design). You will need to find a space and probably hire some trestle tables as you need quite a bit of room to decorate hundreds of cupcakes. On the day, the best way to organise production is to have one to three production lines—each line with a leader (one of your crew). Each of the lines either ganaches, covers or decorates the cupcakes. The crew leaders can rotate volunteers according to skill base and how long they have been on a certain task to help keep them interested.

See also Party Organiser starting on page 96.

EVENT TIMELINE

- Welcome/aprons on (10 mins)
- Cupcake decorating demo × 3 (10 mins) for each production line
- Decorating per person (1 hour for 10 cupcakes)
- Boxing cupcakes for charity (20 mins)
- Prizes (10 mins)
- Boxing two cupcakes for each volunteer and goodbyes (10 mins)

Electric Star Cupcake

EQUIPMENT *(per person)*
For ganaching and covering cupcakes
Small kitchen knife
Cranked palette knife
Plastic jug
Pastry brush
Small rolling pin
Set of circle cutters
Flexi-smoother

For decorating cupcakes
Small rolling pin
Large and small star cutters
Medium paintbrush
Ziplock bags, to store icing

MATERIALS *(per person)*
5 cupcakes
Syrup (page 109)
100 g (3½ oz) ganache
   (page 108)
200 g (7 oz) green fondant
   icing (coverings)
75 g (2½ oz) purple fondant
   icing (stars)
25 g (1 oz) white fondant icing (stars)
Cornflour (cornstarch), in shaker
Edible glitter (optional)

> *For colouring fondant icing
>   see pages 122–3.*

1 Ganache and cover the cupcake with green fondant icing as per instructions on pages 118–20.

2 Knead the purple fondant icing for the large star into a smooth pliable dough and roll out to 3 mm (⅛ inch) thick (Pic a).

3 Using a large star cutter, cut out a star shape (Pic b). Place the star on the cupcake with a dab of water.

4 Roll out the white fondant icing for the small star to 3 mm (⅛ inch) thick and, using a small star cutter, cut out a star shape (Pic c).

5 Carefully place the white star in the centre of the purple star with a dab of water (Pic d).

Optional: Using a medium paintbrush, decorate with edible glitter.

a

b

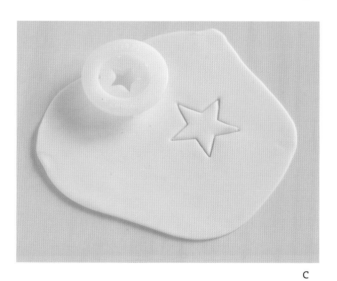

c

d

a

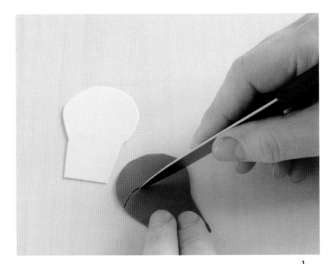

b

c

d

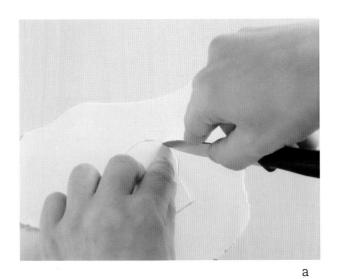

Cupcake Cupcakes

EQUIPMENT (*per person*)

For ganaching and covering cupcakes

Small kitchen knife

Cranked palette knife

Plastic jug

Pastry brush

Small rolling pin

Set of circle cutters

Flexi-smoother

For decorating cupcakes

Small rolling pin

Cupcake template (page 129)

Small sharp knife

Frilling tool

Medium paintbrush

Ziplock bags, to store icing

MATERIALS (*per person*)

5 cupcakes

Syrup (page 109)

100 g (3½ oz) ganache
  (page 108)

200 g (7 oz) red fondant
  icing (coverings)

100 g (3½ oz) white fondant
  icing (cupcake shapes)

100 g (3½ oz) brown fondant
  icing (cupcake tops)

100 g (3½ oz) yellow fondant
  icing (paper cases)

Tiny pinch purple fondant
  icing (for each cherry)

Cornflour (cornstarch), in shaker

> *For colouring fondant icing
>   see pages 122–3.*

1 Ganache and cover the cupcake with red fondant icing as per instructions on pages 118–20. See tips for red icing on page 123.

2 Knead the white fondant icing for the cupcake shape into a smooth pliable dough. Roll out to 3 mm (⅛ inch) thick. Using the cupcake template and a sharp knife, cut out a cupcake shape (Pic a).

3 Smooth the sides of the cupcake shape with warm fingers. Stick the cupcake shape in the centre of the cupcake with a dab of water.

4 Roll out the brown fondant icing for the cupcake shape to 3 mm (¹/₈ inch) thick. Using the cupcake template, cut out another cupcake shape. Cut the cake part in half, using a knife to make a wave shape. This top half will become the icing on your cupcake shape (Pic b). Discard the remainder of the cupcake shape. Attach the cupcake icing to the cupcake icing shape.

5 Roll out the yellow fondant icing for the paper case to 3 mm (⅛ inch) thick. Using the cupcake template, cut another cupcake shape. Cut off the paper case (cupcake base) part (Pic c). Discard remainder of the cupcake shape. Attach the paper case icing to the cupcake icing shape. With the frilling tool mark the indents for the paper case (Pic d).

6 Roll a very small ball of purple fondant icing for the cherry and glue on top of the cupcake shape using a drop of water.

Tiger Hunt

Kids' Party (Ages 4–7)

Okay, I admit it, little kids can be tough customers. The worst complaint I ever had was from a 6 year old when I got Spiderman's eyes wrong on his birthday cake. I can still see that little boy dressed in his Spiderman suit screaming. I have also hosted many birthday parties for my daughter Estelle, which I must admit I have found rather nerve-racking. I mean, let's be honest, we don't want to embarrass our children in front of their friends by giving a lame party. I have done everything from the sports party to the dessert table extravaganza. However, I am sure everyone will agree that kids seem to have fun with whatever activity you propose, because they are kids! Once I worked this out, my focus was on activities that didn't cost a fortune and that made Estelle's party unique—a party that other children would remember. As a party activity, cupcake decorating is successful because it's quick, it has impact, the kids are in control and they can eat the results. It is also a retreat for quieter children. The activity will last for approximately 30 minutes to 1 hour depending on the age and the amount of sugar ingested by the child. The younger children can cut out icing shapes and stick them onto cupcakes with different coloured icing, while older children can also decorate. They can dress up as chefs and most of the tools required come in children's baking kits (which also make good party favours). The cupcake theme can be tailored to the party theme, all the kids can decorate a cupcake for the guest of honour, and children will naturally improvise their designs. It goes without saying that these events are a photographer's delight!

HOW THE PARTY WORKS

The best way to understand how the party works is to start with the end result. Each child will leave the party with at least two cupcakes (one of each design) that they have proudly decorated themselves, and a prize or two. They will use important tools such as small rolling pins, paintbrushes, flexi-smoothers and cake cutters. You can find most of these items in kids' mini baking kits that can be given as take-home gifts. The adults need to ganache and cover the cupcakes and colour the icing ready for little fingers to create their masterpieces. It is advisable to have a trial decorating run before the party so that you can give a brief demonstration before each activity. The designs require no cake decorating experience.

See also Party Organiser starting on page 96.

EVENT TIMELINE

- Welcome/aprons on (5 mins)
- Decorating per child (30 mins for two cupcakes)
- Photos and prizes (10 mins)
- Box cupcakes and goodbyes

Tiger Paws Cupcake

EQUIPMENT *(per person)*

For ganaching and covering cupcakes

Small kitchen knife
Cranked palette knife
Plastic jug
Pastry brush
Small rolling pin
Set of circle cutters
Flexi-smoother

For decorating cupcakes

Medium paintbrush
Flexi-smoother
Ziplock bags, to store icing

MATERIALS *(per person)*

1 cupcake
Syrup (page 109)
20 g (¾ oz) ganache
   (page 108)
40 g (1½ oz) black fondant
   icing (covering)
30 g (1 oz) yellow fondant
   icing (paws)
Cornflour (cornstarch), in shaker

> For colouring fondant icing
> see pages 122–3.

1 Ganache and cover the cupcake with black fondant icing as per instructions on pages 118–20. (*This must be done in advance.*)

2 Pinch off yellow fondant icing for the paws into four pea-sized pieces and one grape-sized piece (Pic a).

3 Roll into balls and then squash flat between your fingers to create four small spots and one larger spot (Pic b).

4 Place very small dabs of water on the cupcake in the shape of a paw print and attach each of the spots (Pic c).

5 When dry, press gently over the top with a flexi-smoother to smooth the spots (Pic d).

a

b

c

d

a

b

c

d

Be a Star Cupcake

EQUIPMENT *(per person)*

For ganaching and covering cupcakes

Small kitchen knife

Cranked palette knife

Plastic jug

Pastry brush

Small rolling pin

Set of circle cutters

Flexi-smoother

For decorating cupcakes

Small rolling pin

Large star cutters

Medium paintbrush

Ziplock bags, to store icing

MATERIALS *(per person)*

1 cupcake

Syrup (page 109)

20 g (¾ oz) ganache
   (page 108)

40 g (1½ oz) blue fondant
   icing (covering)

15 g (½ oz) red fondant icing (star)

Cornflour (cornstarch), in shaker

Edible glitter

> *For colouring fondant icing
>   see pages 122–3.*

1   Ganache and cover the cupcake with blue fondant icing as per instructions on pages 118–20. (*This must be done in advance.*)

2   Knead the red fondant icing for the star into a smooth pliable dough. Roll out to 3 mm (⅛ inch) thick (Pic a).

3   Using a large star cutter, cut out a star shape (Pic b).

4   Place the star on the cupcake with a dab of water (Pic c).

5   When dry, press gently over the top with a flexi-smoother to smooth.

6   Using a medium paintbrush, decorate the red star with glitter (Pic d). See glitter tips on page 125.

Cupcake Challenge TV Show

Kids' Party (Ages 7–12)

I actually had this event forced upon me when I was asked to be a guest judge at my daughter's school for a cake making competition for 8–10 year olds. I seriously doubted whether children would be interested in cake making and I thought the mess and chaos would be horrendous. Imagine my surprise when I turned up to find all the children waiting for me in their culinary teams wearing chef's hats and holding their creations on silver trays. Children had to fulfil judging criteria then had to present their cakes to the judging panel (myself and other parents). I remember my heart broke when a very scruffy looking 8-year-old boy with scabbed knees explained to me his patience and experimentation in getting the decorating just so. His team presented their creation as 'Chocolate Romance' and ultimately won first place. What did the success of the event show me? Just like us, children have been directly influenced by the worldwide food craze and they are familiar with food in a way that our generations were not. Children love an opportunity to work in teams and be creative. It also showed me that given a task, children will often rise to it. I have since replicated this event for children from ages 8–12 and it never fails. It's a lot of organisation, but it is perfect for boys, girls and adults. It is like running your own TV show, except the kids get to be the stars. I must admit I did some mental arithmetic to work out exactly when I would be competing against Mr. Chocolate Romance in the food industry, because I seriously fear I won't stand a chance!

HOW THE PARTY WORKS

This event is themed like a TV show and requires a minimum of eight kids, four in each team. The goal is for each team to decorate 20 cupcakes in one hour using the designs as a template but improvising on those designs. After a 20-minute demo, teams are shown their cupcakes, ganache and equipment and are expected to proceed for the next hour on their own. They are allowed three lifeline questions. The teams that succeed in these events are those that can organise a production line and prioritise their time and resources. This event works best with props (see Extra Pizzazz on page 99).

See also Party Organiser starting on page 96.

COMPETITION RULES

1. Each team must elect a leader
2. Each team must choose a team name
3. Each team has one hour to complete the challenge
4. Each team must decorate 20 cupcakes per team
5. Each team must decorate an equal number of each design
6. Extra points will be awarded for design improvisation
7. Extra points will be awarded for presentation and neatness
8. Bonus points will be awarded for extra cupcakes decorated

EVENT TIMELINE

- Welcome/aprons on (10 mins)
- Cupcake decorating demo (20 mins)
- Competition time per team (1 hour for 20 cupcakes)
- Photos and prizes (15 mins)
- Box cupcakes and goodbyes

Freddy Face Cupcake

EQUIPMENT *(per person)*

For ganaching and covering cupcakes

Small kitchen knife

Cranked palette knife

Plastic jug

Pastry brush

Small rolling pin

Set of circle cutters

Flexi-smoother

For decorating cupcakes

Small rolling pin

Freddy Face template
(page 129)

Small sharp knife

Frilling tool

Medium paintbrush

Ziplock bags, to store icing

MATERIALS *(per person)*

5 cupcakes

Syrup (page 109)

100 g (3½ oz) ganache
(page 108)

200 g (7 oz) white fondant
icing (coverings)

150 g (5½ oz) green fondant
icing (faces)

50 g (1¾ oz) white fondant
icing, extra (eye balls)

25 g (1 oz) black fondant
icing (pupils)

50 g (1¾ oz) red fondant
icing (tongues)

Cornflour (cornstarch), in shaker

> *For colouring fondant icing
> see pages 122–3.*

1 Ganache and cover the cupcake with white fondant icing as per instructions on pages 118–20.

2 Knead the green fondant icing for the face into a smooth pliable dough. Roll out to 3 mm (⅛ inch) thick. Using the Freddy Face template, cut out Freddy Face as per instructions on pages 128–29 (Pic a). Stick face to the top of the cupcake with a little water.

3 Roll two small balls of the extra white fondant icing for the eyeballs and stick on the top of the face with a dab of water (Pic b).

4 With the frilling tool, mark a hole in each eyeball. Roll two small balls of black fondant icing for the pupils and place in the white indentations with a dab of water (Pic c).

5 With the frilling tool, mark two holes for the nose and an indent for the mouth.

6 Roll out the red fondant icing for the tongue to 3 mm (⅛ inch) thick. Using a knife, cut an oval shape and cut the end off. Place the flat end in the mouth using a small dab of water. Pinch the rounded end to a point. Mark the centre line on the tongue using the frilling tool (Pic d).

a

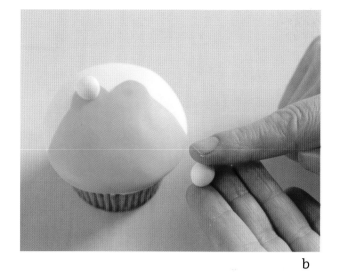

b

c

d

a

b

c

d

Girly Bear Cupcake

EQUIPMENT *(per person)*

For ganaching and covering cupcakes

Small kitchen knife
Cranked palette knife
Plastic jug
Pastry brush
Small rolling pin
Set of circle cutters
Flexi-smoother

For decorating cupcakes

Frilling tool
Medium paintbrush
Ziplock bags, to store icing

MATERIALS *(per person)*

5 cupcakes
Syrup (page 109)
100 g (3½ oz) ganache
 (page 108)
200 g (7 oz) pink fondant
 icing (coverings)
150 g (5½ oz) pale pink
 fondant icing (snouts)
75 g (2½ oz) black fondant
 icing (eyes and noses)
50 g (1¾ oz) pink fondant
 icing, extra (ears)
25 g (1 oz) pale pink fondant
 icing, extra (inside ears)
Red petal dust
Cornflour (cornstarch), in shaker

....
: *For colouring fondant icing* :
:   *see pages 122–3.* :
....

1 Ganache and cover the cupcake with pink fondant icing as per instructions on pages 118–20.

2 Roll out an almond-sized ball of pale pink fondant icing for the snout and stick in the lower half of the face with a dab of water. Using the edge of round cutter or frilling tool, indent the mouth (Pic a).

3 Roll out a small ball of black fondant icing for the nose and stick in the centre top of the snout with a dab of water.

4 With the frilling tool, mark two holes for the eyes. Roll two tiny balls of black fondant icing for the eyes and stick the balls into the indents (Pic b).

5 Roll a pea-sized ball of pink fondant icing for the ears and flatten slightly. Roll out a tiny pinch of the extra pale pink fondant icing for the inner ears, flatten slightly and press into the centre of the pink ear circle (Pic c). Cut the circles in half to form two ears. Sculpt the ovals into the shape of a bear ear using a frilling tool (or the end of a paintbrush). Attach to the cupcake with a dab of water.

6 Mix the red petal dust with a little cornflour (to dilute) and dust on each side of the face with a dry paintbrush to give rosy cheeks (Pic d).

Mini Messengers

Something to Say Party

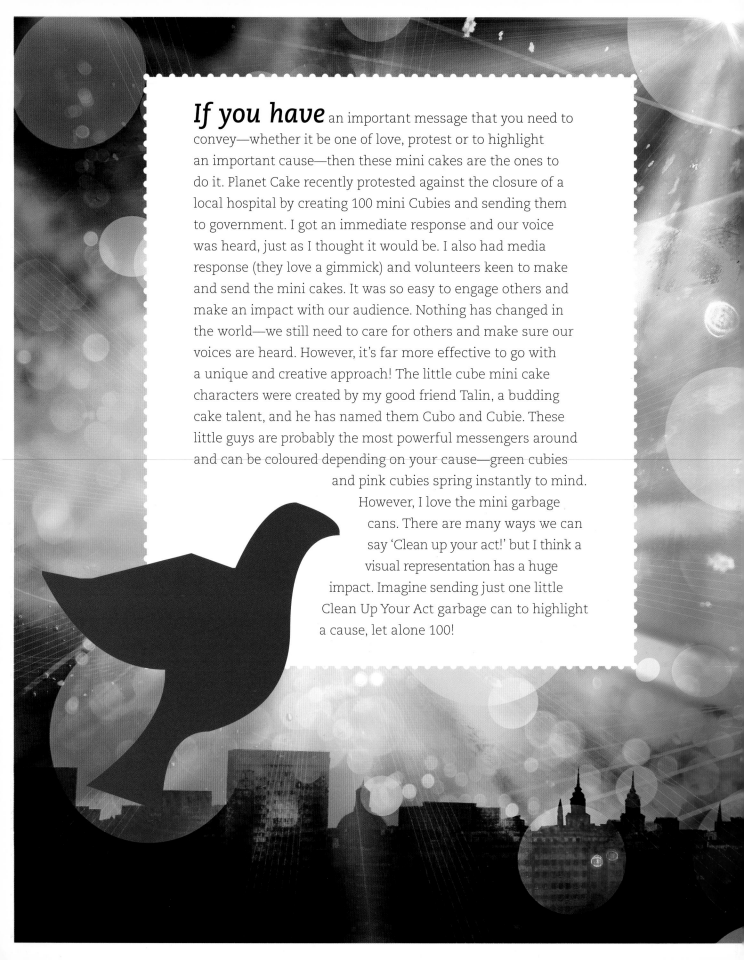

If you have an important message that you need to convey—whether it be one of love, protest or to highlight an important cause—then these mini cakes are the ones to do it. Planet Cake recently protested against the closure of a local hospital by creating 100 mini Cubies and sending them to government. I got an immediate response and our voice was heard, just as I thought it would be. I also had media response (they love a gimmick) and volunteers keen to make and send the mini cakes. It was so easy to engage others and make an impact with our audience. Nothing has changed in the world—we still need to care for others and make sure our voices are heard. However, it's far more effective to go with a unique and creative approach! The little cube mini cake characters were created by my good friend Talin, a budding cake talent, and he has named them Cubo and Cubie. These little guys are probably the most powerful messengers around and can be coloured depending on your cause—green cubies and pink cubies spring instantly to mind. However, I love the mini garbage cans. There are many ways we can say 'Clean up your act!' but I think a visual representation has a huge impact. Imagine sending just one little Clean Up Your Act garbage can to highlight a cause, let alone 100!

HOW THE EVENT WORKS

You need to set a target for mini messengers, but for novices one mini cake per person should be ample. Ask your volunteers for a donation to cover the cost of materials, for example $10 each. Once you have set your target, you will know the numbers of volunteers required and can enlist your army. Set decorating shifts of 1½ hours. It is too much to expect beginners to be decorating for hours on end. In 1½ hours you can estimate that each volunteer should be able to decorate at least one mini cake. To keep volunteers excited you can set prizes and keep a cake tally. Box them neatly together with the message they are carrying and send them to the recipients. I suggest you take photos and create your own Facebook page. Everyone loves watching the minis come to life and go on their mission!

See also Party Organiser starting on page 96.

EVENT TIMELINE

- Welcome/aprons on (10 mins)
- Mini cake decorating demo (10 mins)
- Mini cake decorating per person (1½ hours for one mini cake)
- Photos and prizes (10 mins)
- Boxing and mission begins

Cubo and Cubie

EQUIPMENT *(per person)*
Small kitchen knife
Pastry brush
Rolling pin
Scissors or pizza cutter
Paintbrush
Flexi-smoother
Pasta machine (for general use)

MATERIALS *(per person)*
80 g (2¾ oz) fudge (page 106)
60 g (2¼ oz) yellow fondant
   icing (covering)
10 g (¼ oz) white fondant
   icing (eyeballs)
5 g (⅛ oz) black fondant
   icing (pupils)
10 g (¼ oz) yellow fondant
   icing, extra (nose)
10 g (¼ oz) yellow fondant
   icing, extra (mouth)
40 g (1½ oz) yellow fondant
   icing (feet)
Toothpicks (feet)
Cornflour (cornstarch), in shaker

For colouring fondant icing see pages 122–3.

1 Cut fudge into two pieces, each 4 cm (1½ inch) square × 2 cm (1 inch) thick (Pic a). Brush the two pieces of fudge with a little water and stack them together to form a cube.

2 Brush the top with a little water. Roll the yellow fondant icing for the covering in the pasta machine on #1 setting (Pic b). Cut a square to cover the top of the cube. Place on top and smooth the edges. Repeat to cover the bottom of the cube (Pic c).

3 Brush the sides of the cube with a little water. Roll remaining yellow fondant icing in the pasta machine on #1 setting. Cut a strip about 18 × 6 cm (7 × 2½ inch) long. Roll the icing strip around the cube, starting from the middle of one side (Pic d). Trim and smooth the joining line with a warm finger. Trim the top edge of the icing with a sharp knife and smooth all the edges.

4 For the eyeballs, pinch a ball of white fondant icing the size of a pea. Split it in half, roll into two balls and squash flat. Stretch the balls slightly to form ovals. Stick the eyes on the cube with a dab of water (Pic e). Repeat this process with some black fondant icing, starting with a ball half the size of a pea. Stick in the lower half of the eyes with a dab of water.

5 Roll the yellow fondant icing for the nose into a ball and attach with a dab of water. Roll the yellow icing for the mouth into a thin sausage. Cut the sausage in half and then place onto the face to form lips.

6 To make the feet, take about 20 g (¾ oz) of fondant icing and form two 1.3 × 1.5 cm (½ × ⅝ inch) shapes with warm fingers and pinch the base of each to make feet. Place a toothpick in each leg and insert the feet into the body (Pic f).

To make Cubie (page 87), follow steps 1-6 (using white fondant icing instead of yellow and making the feet smaller). Use black colour paste mixed with a little cake decorating alcohol to paint the eyelashes. Mix red petal dust with a little cornflour and dust on each side of the face with a dry paintbrush to give rosy cheeks. Use pink colour paste mixed with a little cake decorating alcohol to paint the toenails.

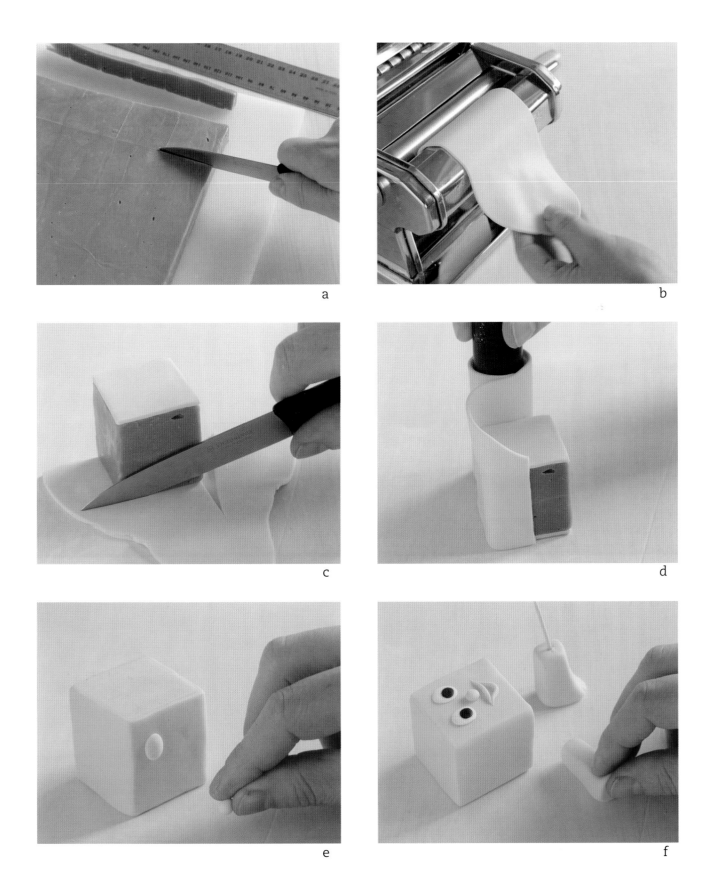

a

b

c

d

e

f

Clean Up Your Act!

EQUIPMENT (*per person*)
Small rolling pin
Pastry brush
Small kitchen knife
Circle cutters
Medium paintbrush
Flexi-smoother

MATERIALS (*per person*)
100 g (3½ oz) fudge (page 106)
5 g (⅛ oz) fudge, extra
80 g (2¾ oz) fondant icing
   (any colour)
Cornflour (cornstarch), in shaker

> *For colouring fondant icing*
> *see pages 122–3.*

1 Mould the fudge into a cylinder shape, tapering slightly at one end to form the base of the rubbish can (Pic a).

2 Knead three-quarters of the fondant icing into a smooth pliable dough. Roll out to 3 mm (⅛ inch) thick. Brush the cylinder all over with water. Roll the icing around the can.

3 Trim and smooth the joining line with a warm finger (Pic b). Trim the top edge (wider end) of the icing with a sharp knife.

4 For the lid, roll some of the leftover fondant icing to 3 mm (⅛ inch) thick. Using a circle cutter, cut a circle large enough to cover the top (wider end) of the cylinder.

5 Brush the top with water and place the circle on top and smooth the edges (Pic c). Repeat with a smaller circle to make the cover for the bottom of the can.

6 Using a frilling tool, mark the rim and indents on the lid (Pic d).

7 Lay the can on its side and, using the end of the paintbrush, push indents around the can (Pic e).

8 Pinch a piece of fondant icing the size of half a pea and place in the centre of the lid. Roll a small pinch of icing into a strip to form the handles. Cut in half and press each end onto the lid with a dab of water (Pic f).

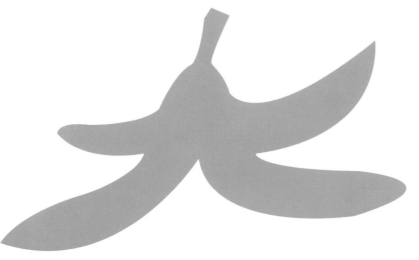

Party
Planning

Organiser Basics

PREPARATION TIMELINE

Good event planning results in fantastic cakes. Here are some suggestions for making your event a success. When considering the type of event you want to hold, a good first step is to have a vision of what this event means to you—your concept, purpose and goals. Then consider these in light of the needs of your audience. Next, read the chapter of the event you wish to replicate and start putting it all together. See the suggested four-week timetable on page 98.

CONDUCTING DEMONSTRATIONS

Giving a cupcake demonstration can be fun. You might find it daunting to give demonstrations, but with a little advance preparation, anyone can do it. I advise that you give demonstrations for each step of the decorating process.

- List your demonstrations for each step.
- List equipment for your demonstrations. Your list should include everything.
- Practise your demonstrations. You may want to use the notes at the back of this book or note cards. Practise each demo exactly as you will give it. This is where you can make changes and adjustments in your presentation.

- Perform your demonstrations. Some find it hard to speak in public. Preparation and prctice will help you get over this fear.
- Review your demonstrations. This is helpful if you plan to do any more. Make notes on areas you can improve. Ask your audience if there is anything further they would like you to cover.

SETTING UP TEMPORARY WORKSTATIONS

It is not necessary to have a gourmet kitchen to host your cupcake shower or event. However, you will require bench space, at least 100 cm (about 40 inch) per guest. You will need a microwave, an area to wash hands and space for cupcakes, which take up more room than you think.

In a perfect world you would have three separate decorating stations for each of the three primary activities—ganaching, covering and decorating. However, if you don't have enough space or tables for each station then make sure you clean thoroughly in between.

For Melanie's cupcake shower (page 16), I hired three trestle tables that were perfect. We set them up outside in an undercover area so we were able to make as much mess as we wanted.

Ganaching Station

Equipment:	Small kitchen knife, palette knife, plastic jug, pastry brush
Materials:	Ganache, cupcakes, syrup
Required:	Area to wash hands, microwave
Warning:	Ganache stains carpets

Covering Station

Equipment:	Large rolling pin, flexi-smoother, knives, circle cutters, ziplock bags
Materials:	Ganached cupcakes, colour paste, icing, cornflour (cornstarch), syrup
Required:	Clean countertop (if you are using the ganaching table, take the time to make sure it is very clean)
Warning:	No water!

Decorating Station

Equipment:	Small kitchen knife, cutters, paintbrushes, small rolling pin
Materials:	Covered cupcakes, colour pastes, edible glitter
Required:	Chairs for decorators who need to sit down; a dining room table or trestle table
Warning:	Make sure any carpet is covered

BOXING CAKES

Packaging is important, particularly if the cakes are to be sent to individuals to promote a charity or for fundraising. Choose small clear plastic boxes—these are available at craft stores in the party section and also at cake decorating shops. They can be tied with pretty ribbons with an attached message, or labels promoting your event can be stuck to the outside. Noodle boxes are also great for transporting individual cupcakes or mini cakes and are available in a variety of sizes.

For kids, cupcakes often fit neatly into cardboard party favour or candy baskets available at craft stores in the party section.

For 10 or so cupcakes, plastic containers are available from some supermarkets or variety stores. These hold around 10 or 12 cupcakes in a two-tier container with a sealable lid and handle.

If you have a large number of cakes to transport, stackable flat trays are best. These can often be borrowed from cake shops or catering companies.

FOUR-WEEK TIMETABLE

TIME LINE	PREPARATION	NOTES
Week 1	Plan venue and allocate responsibilities Choose cupcake designs (all designs are interchangeable between events) Cupcake trial	If you are working in a team, now is the time to assign tasks and baking, etc. Now is the time to make a decision as to whether you want to keep all of our design choices or make some of your own.
Week 2	Hire tables Book a baker Collate equipment and materials	Party hire is fantastic but get organised. If you don't have the time or facilities to bake cupcakes or make fudge, find a supplier. Decide on the number you require and remember that you will need some spares. Some cake decorating supplies can take time to source and ordering them online is much cheaper. There may be a shop that is happy to lend or donate for a charity event.
Week 3	Make flexi-smoothers Theme and prizes, etc.	See Glossary on page 132. See Extra Pizzazz opposite.
Week 4	Final preparations	
Two days before event	Bake or collect cupcakes	
One day before event	Prepare the venue and set up decorating stations	Make sure your have everything you require, including room in your freezer, bench space, equipment, and peace and quiet. Re-read your instructions and smile!

EXTRA PIZZAZZ

Try one or more of the following to add pizzazz to your event:

- Start a Facebook page. (Remember to keep event address details private and only supply an email address for contact.)
- Have aprons made for the cake event.
- Introduce logo or wedding colours by using different colour pastes.
- Create a special meaning for your event by choosing a charity to donate your cupcakes to, such as a women's refuge, food charity or local hospital.
- Arrange a photographer.
- Make the group photo extra special by setting up a dessert table with cake stands and a backdrop to display the final results.
- Have a large clock to 'count down' the time for competitions.
- Keep a visible cake tally so that decorators can see their progress.
- Award prizes for Most Creative, Most Professional and Competition Winner!

FOOD HANDLING SAFETY TIPS

- Wash hands at regular intervals, if not wearing gloves.
- When washing hands always use a clean dish towel or kitchen paper that will only be used once.
- Keep fingernails trimmed and scrubbed to prevent the spread of disease.
- Tie back hair, wear a hair net or hat to keep hair from contaminating food.
- Wear shoes that cover the whole foot to prevent accidents in the kitchen —no thongs, flip-flops or sandals.
- Always use clean utensils and never use utensils that have been used for raw food with cooked food.

WORKSHEET

Name: ....

Notes: ....

....

....

Ganaching the cupcakes

1 Using a sharp knife, trim your cupcakes to achieve a relatively flat and uniform dome. Brush the top of the cupcakes liberally with syrup. This will help to prevent them from drying out.

2 Make sure the ganache is at room temperature and that you can whip it with your palette knife. If it is hard, place the ganache in the microwave for 10- to 20-second intervals until it reaches a soft pliable consistency.

4 Using a palette knife, apply a dollop of ganache (about 20–30 g/¾–1 oz) on the dome of the cupcake.

5 Spread the ganache across the whole cupcake as if you were smoothing peanut butter, making sure not to dirty the paper cases with the ganache.

6 Once all the cupcakes are roughly ganached, dip the pallete knife in a jug of boiling water and smooth the surface of each cupcake.

Tip: If you find smoothing your cupcake with a palette knife too challenging, try using a very clean finger.

Name: ....

Notes: ....

....

....

Covering the cupcakes

1 Lightly brush the cupcakes with syrup. Don't soak them.

2 Knead the fondant icing into a smooth pliable dough. Roll out to 3 mm (⅛ inch) thick and cut circles of the required size (match circle cutter required to top of cupcake).

3 Cut all the circles you need and store them in a ziplock bag to stop them drying out.

4 Remove one fondant icing circle at a time and place it on top of the ganached cupcake, as per the photograph.

5 Using a flexi-smoother, smooth the icing on the cupcake.

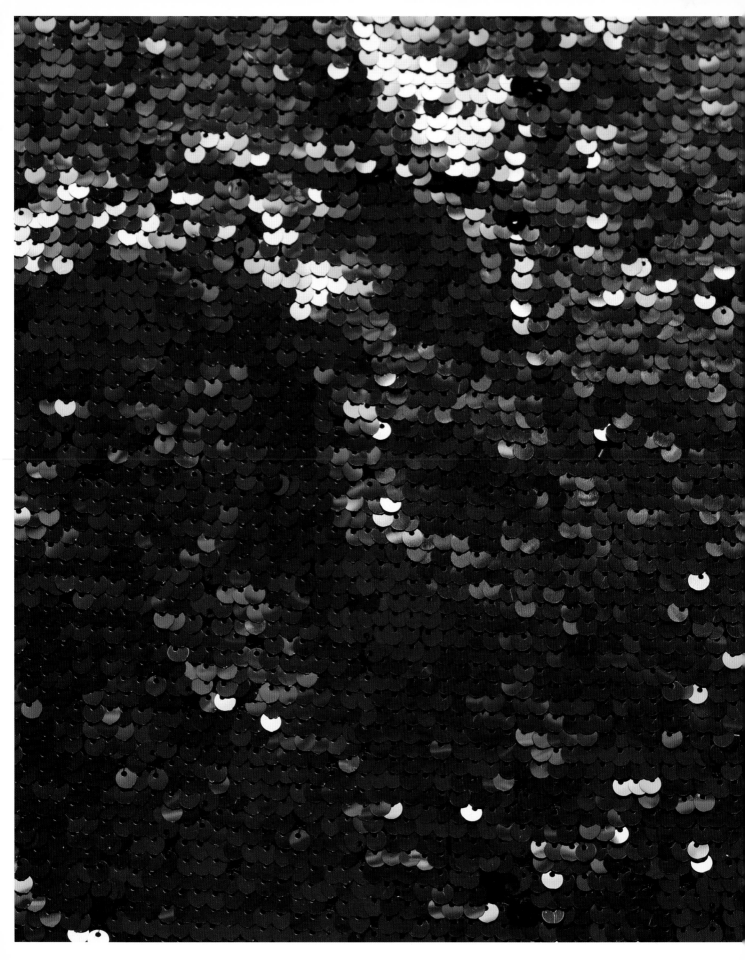

Recipes

Vanilla Cupcakes

Makes 12

Preparation time: 15 minutes
  (cooling)
Cooking time: 25–30 minutes

175 g (6 oz) butter, at room temperature
165 g (5¾ oz/¾ cup) caster (superfine) sugar
½ teaspoon natural vanilla extract
2 eggs, at room temperature
110 g (3¾ oz/¾ cup) self-raising flour
150 g (5½ oz/1 cup) plain
  (all-purpose) flour
160 ml (5½ fl oz/⅔ cup) buttermilk

1 Preheat the oven to 180°C (350°F/Gas 4). Line
   the holes of a 12-hole 80 ml (2½ fl oz/⅓ cup)
   muffin tin with paper cases.

2 Beat the butter, sugar and vanilla in
   a medium bowl using an electric mixer
   until light and fluffy.

3 Beat the eggs into the butter mixture one at
   a time. Add half the sifted flours and half
   the buttermilk, and mix on low speed until
   just combined. Mix in the remaining flours
   and buttermilk.

4 Divide the mixture evenly among the paper
   cases. Gently smooth the tops (this will help
   the cupcakes rise evenly).

5 Bake for 25–30 minutes or until lightly
   golden and cooked when tested with
   a skewer. Allow cupcakes to stand for
   5 minutes in tin before transferring to
   a wire rack to cool.

CHOCOLATE CUPCAKES

Reduce the plain (all-purpose) flour to 110 g
(3¾ oz/¾ cup). Sift 30 g (1 oz/¼ cup) sifted
unsweetened cocoa powder and ¼ teaspoon
bicarbonate of soda (baking soda) with
the flours.

Gluten-free Cupcakes

Makes 12
Preparation time: 15 minutes
  (cooling)
Cooking time: 25–30 minutes

175 g (6 oz) butter, at room temperature
165 g (5¾oz/¾ cup) caster (superfine) sugar
½ teaspoon natural vanilla extract
2 eggs, at room temperature
140 g (5 oz/1 cup) gluten-free
  self-raising flour
140 g (5 oz/1 cup) gluten-free
  plain (all-purpose) flour
160 ml (5½ fl oz/⅔ cup) buttermilk

1 Preheat the oven to 180°C (350°F/Gas 4). Line
   the holes of a 12-hole 80 ml (2½ fl oz/⅓ cup)
   muffin tin with paper cases.

2 Beat the butter, sugar and vanilla in a
   medium bowl using an electric mixer until
   light and fluffy.

3 Beat the eggs into the butter mixture one
   at a time. Add half the sifted flours and
   half the buttermilk, and mix on low speed
   until just combined. Mix in the remaining
   flours and buttermilk.

4 Divide the mixture evenly among the paper
   cases. Gently smooth the tops (this will help
   the cupcakes rise evenly).

5 Bake for 25–30 minutes or until lightly
   golden and cooked when tested with
   a skewer. Allow cupcakes to stand for
   5 minutes in tin before transferring to
   a wire rack to cool.

CUPCAKE TIPS

- Start testing the cupcakes 2 minutes
  before the end of baking time. Once
  they give a light resistance to touch,
  you can start testing them with a
  toothpick or skewer. The tester must
  come out clean, with absolutely no wet
  mixture and no crumbs clinging to it.

- Store the vanilla and chocolate
  cupcakes in a sealed airtight container
  in the fridge for up to 3 days, and the
  gluten-free cakes for up to 1 day. All
  cupcakes can also be frozen for up to
  3 months. Bring to room temperature
  before decorating.

- The most important thing to consider
  when making cakes for events is to
  ensure that the cupcakes are firm and
  not straight from the oven. It is best if
  the cupcakes are baked the day before.
  White chocolate cupcakes are usually
  the best to use as they are matched
  with white chocolate ganache that is
  easier for novices to use as there is less
  risk of it staining the paper cases.

Caramel Fudge

Makes 500 g (1 lb 2 oz) or 25 × 8 cm (10 × 3¼ inch) slab

Preparation time: 10 minutes
Cooking time: 15 minutes

395 g (14 oz) can sweetened condensed milk
150 g (5½ oz/⅔ cup) brown sugar
75 g (approx 2½ oz/⅓ cup caster (superfine) sugar
2 tablespoons glucose syrup
2 tablespoons golden syrup (light corn syrup)
80 g (2¾ oz) butter, in small cubes

1 Grease a 25 x 8 cm (10 x 3¼ inch) rectangular cake pan. Line the base and sides with baking paper, extending it by 2 cm (1 inch) above the two long sides.

2 Place the condensed milk, sugars, glucose syrup, golden syrup and butter in a medium heavy-based saucepan over low heat. Cook, stirring, without boiling, for 3–4 minutes or until the sugar has dissolved.

3 Increase the heat to medium and bring to the boil while stirring. Cook, stirring constantly, for 8–10 minutes or until the mixture thickens and comes away from side of the saucepan. Remove from the heat.

4 Pour the hot mixture into a small mixing bowl. Using an electric mixer, beat for 3–4 minutes or until mixture has cooled slightly and is thick. Spoon the fudge into the prepared pan and smooth the top with a spatula. Stand for 30 minutes. Cover with plastic wrap and refrigerate for 4 hours or until firm.

Note: A heavy-based saucepan will help prevent the fudge from sticking to the base and burning. Store the fudge in an airtight container in the fridge for up to 2 weeks.

FUDGE TIPS

- Do not bring fudge to the boil until the sugar is fully dissolved. Boiling the mixture with undissolved sugar will cause it to crystallise.

- Fudge must be stirred constantly to prevent it from sticking to the base of the pan.

- For ease of cleaning, pour boiling water into the pan and mixing bowl. Stand for 2–3 minutes and then rinse away the dissolved fudge residue.

- For larger quantities, the fudge recipe can be doubled and cooked in a larger saucepan. Cooking times will increase by 3–4 minutes in total. Pour the fudge into a 20 cm (8 inch) square cake pan lined with baking paper. Leave enough paper up the sides to enable you to lift out the fudge.

- Store the fudge in an airtight container in a cool, dry place for up to 2 weeks. In hot, humid weather, store in the fridge.

- Use warm, dry hands to mould fudge into the desired shape.

Ganache

Makes about 480 g (1 lb 1 oz/1¼ cups),
enough for 24 cupcakes

Preparation time: 10 minutes
Cooking time: 5 minutes (overnight standing)

The ideal chocolate for making ganache is a
couverture variety with a cocoa content of 53–63
per cent. In cold weather, you might have to add
a touch more cream so that the ganache doesn't
set too hard.

WHITE GANACHE
325 g (11½ oz) white chocolate, finely chopped
150 ml (5 fl oz) cream

DARK GANACHE
300 g (10½ oz) dark chocolate, finely chopped
150 ml (5 fl oz) cream

1 To make either the white or dark ganache, put
the chocolate in a medium heatproof bowl.

2 Put the cream in a saucepan and bring just
to a simmer. Pour the cream over the
chocolate and stir with a balloon whisk until
the ganache is smooth.

3 Cool completely. Cover and leave to firm
overnight at room temperature.

Microwave method
1 Put the chocolate and cream in a microwave-
safe bowl and heat for 1 minute on HIGH
power. Remove from microwave and stir with
a balloon whisk. Repeat, heating in 10–20
second bursts, stirring between each, until
the ganache is smooth.

2 Cool completely. Cover and leave to firm
overnight at room temperature.

GANACHE TIPS
- At Planet Cake, we use either white or
dark chocolate ganache under the
fondant icing on all our cupcakes. We
use white ganache with vanilla and
citrus-flavoured cupcakes, and when
covering cupcakes with pale-coloured
fondant icing; and dark ganache on
chocolate and nut-based cupcakes.
Note: White ganache is less stable than
dark in hot weather and will not set
as firmly.
- Avoid using dark chocolate with a cocoa
content of more than 63 per cent to make
dark ganache. It is more likely to burn
when heated, and separates easily. It may
also be too bitter in contrast to the sweet
fondant icing, and will set very hard, as it
contains very little cocoa butter.
- We use pure cream (single cream), not
thickened or thick (double) cream, when
making ganache. A cream with a lower fat
content (but not low-fat) is best as it won't
thicken when mixed.
- Ganache will keep for about 1 week in an
airtight container in the fridge, so check
the use-by date of the cream you are
using. It also freezes well if you want to
make a large batch. Freeze it in small
containers so you can thaw just the
quantity needed.
- Always bring ganache to room
temperature before using.
- If your ganache needs reheating to
soften it, place the amount you need in
a microwave-safe dish and heat in
5-second bursts on MEDIUM power,
stirring in between until it reaches the
desired consistency.
- Allow about 20 g (¾ oz) ganache for
each cupcake.

Royal icing

Makes about 270 g (9½ oz/1 cup)

Preparation time: 10 minutes

Achieving just the right consistency for royal icing can be difficult. For piping with tubes, you will need 'soft peak' royal icing—when lifted from the bowl with a spatula, the peak will stand up but droop over slightly at the tip, like uncooked meringue. **Note:** Fondant icing (recipe page 110) is used throughout this book. Royal icing is an alternative.

250–300 g (9–10½ oz/2–2½ cups) pure icing
   (confectioner's) sugar, sifted
1 egg white
2–4 drops lemon juice or white vinegar

1   Put 250 g (9 oz/2 cups) icing sugar, egg white and lemon juice or vinegar in a bowl and beat with an electric mixer on medium–high speed for 5 minutes for 'soft peaks' (less if you want it firmer). If too soft, beat in a little more sifted icing sugar.

2   Store in an airtight container in a cool place (but don't refrigerate) for up to 4 days.

Syrup

Makes about 160 ml
(5¼ fl oz/⅔ cup)

Preparation time: 5 minutes

105 g (3¾ oz/⅓ cup) apricot jam
2 teaspoons orange liqueur (optional)

1   Whisk the jam with 100 ml (3½ fl oz/⅓ cup) boiling water until smooth.

2   Strain through a fine sieve to remove any lumps. Stir in the liqueur, if using.

Fondant Icing

Makes about 1.25 kg (2 lb 12 oz)

Preparation time: 15 minutes
Cooking time: 5 minutes

At Planet Cake, we don't make our own fondant icing, as we find the commercial varieties convenient and often more reliable to use. But if you do need a recipe, this one is courtesy of our friend Greg Cleary—a great cake decorator.

15 g (½ oz) powdered gelatine
125 ml (4 fl oz/½ cup) liquid glucose
25 ml (5 teaspoons) glycerine
1 kg (2 lb 4 oz) pure icing (confectioner's) sugar
2 drops flavour extract (optional)

1   Sprinkle the gelatine over 60 ml (2 fl oz/¼ cup) water in a small heatproof bowl. Leave to stand for 3 minutes or until the gelatine is spongy.

2   Place the bowl over a saucepan of simmering water and stir until the gelatine dissolves. Add the glucose and glycerine and stir until melted. Strain through a fine sieve if the mixture is lumpy.

3   Sift the icing sugar into a large bowl, make a well in the centre and pour in the warm gelatine mixture. Use a wooden spoon until it becomes too difficult to stir. Tip the mixture out onto a bench, add the flavouring extract, if using, and knead with dry hands for 3–5 minutes or until it forms a smooth, pliable dough.

4   Wrap the fondant well in plastic wrap or place in a ziplock bag and store in an airtight container in a cool place (but do not refrigerate).

FONDANT ICING TIPS

- Fondant icing can dry out very quickly, so it is important to work quickly to avoid your icing becoming cracked and difficult to use.

- Never use icing that is too dry or over-kneaded; this will make the icing on the cakes crack very easily.

- NEVER EVER refrigerate icing when it is on a cake. Fondant will sweat in the fridge. Once the cupcakes are covered, they should be stored in a cool place (about 20°C/68°F).

- Never ice cupcakes straight from the fridge. For a professional finish, always bring chilled cakes to room temperature before covering.

- When you are not using your icing (even for a minute), put it in a good-quality sealed plastic bag to avoid it drying out. Any excess or leftover icing is best stored the same way or wrapped in plastic wrap and then in a sealed airtight container. Follow the manufacturer's instructions on how to store your particular brand of purchased icing. We store ours at room temperature.

- Store cornflour in a shaker and use to prevent fondant icing sticking to the work surface or your hands.

- Hot hands may make your fondant icing sticky. Don't be tempted to over-use cornflour, which will dry the icing. Cool your hands under cold water and keep cornflour to a light sprinkle.

- Weather will also affect fondant icing. Humidity will make the icing sticky and very cold weather will make it as hard as a rock.

- Always work the icing in small amounts and try to get above the icing when you knead it on the bench. If you are short, stand on a step stool so you can use your body weight to help you knead. If you try to knead large amounts of icing, you will put undue pressure on your wrists and make the job very difficult.

- Kneading icing is not like kneading dough: if you keep pummelling, it will stick to the board and become unmanageable. Treat fondant icing a bit like playdough and keep folding it in until it is smooth and warm to use, but not sticking to the bench.

- To use fondant icing for modelling, knead 1 teaspoon Tylose powder into 500 g (1 lb 2 oz) fondant until thoroughly combined.

Basics

Equipment

The best thing about decorating cakes is that the list of equipment and materials required is fairly basic. Most of it can be found either at online cake decorating specialists or at your local cake decorating store and much of it may already be in your kitchen or art box. Before you begin, take the time to look at the following lists of equipment and materials that you'll need to start decorating the cupcakes and mini cakes in this book.

1	Spatula	(Not pictured)
2	Large rolling pin	Pasta machine
3	Tracing paper	Stitching tool
4	Piping bag	Pizza cutter
5	Frilling tool	Drinking straws
6	Fine paintbrush	Toothpicks
7	Medium paintbrushes	
8	Ruler	
9	Coupler	
10	Shaped cutters	
11	Scissors	
12	Ziplock bags	
13	Circle cutters	
14	Piping tip	
15	Plastic paint palette	
16	Cranked palette knife	
17	Small rolling pin	
18	Pastry brush	
19	Small kitchen knife	
20	Flour shaker	
21	Flexi-smoother	

1

2

3

4

5

6

7

4

8

9

10

Materials

1 Liquid glucose
2 Cornflour (cornstarch)
3 White lustre dust
4 Edible glitter
5 Edible silver lustre dust
6 Edible gold lustre dust

7 Pink petal dust
8 Fondant icing
9 Cupcakes
10 Syrup
11 Ganache
12 Colour paste

13 Royal icing
14 Red and black
    fondant icing
15 Cake decorating alcohol

Techniques

GANACHING CUPCAKES

At Planet Cake, we ganache our cupcakes to help extend their life span and ensure that they are moist and delicious. Ganache also builds up the surface of the cupcakes, so that they are all perfectly uniform in spite of any imperfections that may have happened during the baking process.

1. Make your ganache (page 108) and allow it to stand overnight at room temperature to firm. If the ganache is too hard when you are ready to use it, heat it in short bursts in the microwave until it reaches the consistency of smooth peanut butter. If you don't have a microwave, put the ganache in a saucepan over low heat, stirring constantly and making sure not to heat it too much.

2. Trim the cupcake tops (optional). If your cupcakes have spilled over their paper cases during baking or are uneven, trim the tops with a sharp knife to make sure they all have a similar height and proportion. Keep in mind it is very difficult to ice a high-domed cupcake, so make sure they are not too high.

3. Brush the top of the cupcakes liberally with syrup (page 109). This will help to prevent them from drying out (Pic a).

4. Using a palette knife, spread approximately 2 teaspoons of ganache across the top of the cupcake, being careful not to touch the paper case, particularly if you are using dark ganache (Pics b, c).

5. Allow the ganache to become firm to the touch before covering with fondant icing (Pic d). If it is a warm day you can place your cakes in the fridge for about 5 minutes.

a

b

c

d

TIP

- When estimating the total amount of ganache needed for covering your cakes, you should allow about 20 g (¾ oz) ganache per cupcake.

TIMING GUIDELINE

At Planet Cake, we use the following timing guideline when covering our cupcakes:

1 Bake your cupcakes and allow to cool (at least 30 minutes). They can be frozen at this stage.

2 Trim and ganache the cupcakes.

3 Set aside for 4 hours or until ganache is firm to the touch.

4 Cover with fondant icing and decorate.

COVERING CUPCAKE

It is very important to learn how to cover cupcakes professionally—practice makes perfect. By the time you have covered a few batches of cupcakes, they will start to look better than most of the cupcakes you can buy commercially. Don't be put off by a bumpy first attempt.

First ganache your cupcakes and check that the ganache is firm before you attempt to cover the cupcakes with rolled fondant. The better the ganache preparation, the better the finished cupcakes will look.

1. Wipe your bench clean and make sure it is dry. Knead the fondant icing to a pliable dough, using just a sprinkle of cornflour if it sticks. Making sure the icing is smooth, roll it into a ball and flatten it with the palm of your hand to about 4 cm (1½ inch) thick.

2. Sprinkle some cornflour on your bench and roll out the icing, starting from the centre and rolling a couple of times in one direction. Turn the icing, and repeat the process. If your bench gets sticky, use a bit more cornflour, but never use cornflour on top of the icing. Keep on rolling and turning this way until the icing is about 3 mm (¹/₈ inch) thick.

a

b

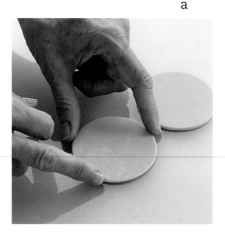

c

d

3. Use a cutter the same size as, or slightly larger than, your cupcakes to cut out the number of discs you need to cover the cakes (Pic a). At Planet Cake, we use a 7 cm (2¾ inch) round cutter. Cover the discs with plastic wrap to prevent them from drying out while cutting out the remainder.

4. Working with one cupcake at a time, brush the ganached cake all over with syrup (page 109). This will help the fondant stick (Pic b).

5. Turn one of the icing discs over and use your fingertip to smooth the edge (Pic c).

6. Turn the disc the right way up and place on top of the cupcake. Gently manipulate the icing so it sits perfectly on the surface of the cupcake.

7. Use a flexi-smoother to smooth the icing disc (Pic d).

- It is possible to decorate some cupcake discs in advance of covering the cake. Follow all of the instructions for covering a cupcake, with the exception of placing the cover on the cake. Decorate the discs separately and place them on the cupcake later if you wish, following the same instructions for placing them. This only works if you have flat cupcake tops; it does not work for domed cupcakes.

- One of our tricks at Planet Cake is to use a pasta machine for rolling out icing. It can be easier than using a traditional rolling pin to get an even thickness. Make sure you knead and roll the icing out first, with a small rolling pin, before feeding it into the pasta machine. And remember to keep the machine clean, especially after using strong colours.

GLUING ICING

There is nothing fancy about gluing icing together, but it can be confusing. Icing is made of sugar and so will readily 'glue' to itself with water alone. You can also use piping gel (page 134) instead of water; apply water or gel using a paintbrush when gluing decorations, to be more accurate. You can also use a dab of royal icing, but it should be the same colour as the fondant it is being applied to, and used very sparingly.

1. Make a very light line or dab of water or gel where the icing needs to be glued (Pic a).

2. Hold the icing piece in place for a few minutes to see if it sets (Pic b). A small sharp utensil to hold and press together is useful for very small pieces/body parts.

Always use a dab of water or gel to secure one piece of icing to another, even when you are also using a skewer or wire for support.

If you haven't applied enough water or gel, you can always add a little more, but if you apply too much, you may end up with a sodden mess.

a

b

COLOURING FONDANT ICING

The important thing to remember when colouring icing to cover cupcakes is to add just a little of the concentrated icing colour at a time, until you arrive at the exact shade you want. Always make sure you have enough coloured icing for all your cupcakes, as matching the original colour can sometimes be an impossible task!

1. Begin with a kneadable amount of white fondant icing, the concentrated icing colour and disposable gloves (Pic a). There are many different brands and types of icing colour and it is easy to become confused. We recommend an icing colour paste, rather than liquid, to colour rolled fondant icing. The gloves are optional, but will keep your hands stain-free.

2. Add a dot of colour to the fondant. Using a toothpick or palette knife, add small dots of icing colour at a time. You can make more elaborate colours by mixing different icing colours together (Pic b). We suggest using a colour wheel as a guide.

3. Knead in the colour paste until the colour is evenly blended, adding a little more colour if needed (Pics c, d). The best way to test whether the colour is blended is to cut the icing in half; it should not be a

a

b

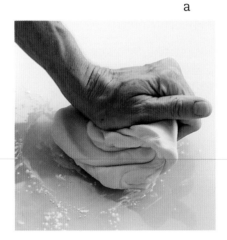

c

d

swirl, but rather a solid colour all the way through.

Intense colours

When making deep colours, such as black, brown, red, orange or royal blue, use icing colour pastes or liquids in larger amounts than normal. It is best to make coloured icing the day before it is needed. The icing will be exceptionally soft (due both to the large amount of colour pigment needed and the amount of kneading required to thoroughly blend it in), so standing it overnight will

help firm it up, making it easier to work with. (See also Red and black icing, opposite.)

Fading

After the icing is coloured, you need to protect the colours from fading. Pinks, purples and blues are especially susceptible to fading out, even in a couple of hours. Pink and mauve can be reduced to almost white when exposed to sunlight; purples to blues; blues to grey. Be careful to protect the icing from light, by covering the cakes with a cloth or placing them in a cake box.

RED AND BLACK ICING

Red- and black-coloured icing can be difficult to make and challenging to work with, because so much colour pigment is required to make an intense colour. In addition, once the icing is coloured successfully, it is very soft and sticky due to the amount of colour required to make it.

To avoid sticky icing, always make red or black icing the day before using it, to allow the colour to be absorbed and the icing to harden. If the icing is still too soft and keeps sticking to the bench, knead in a little sifted icing sugar to dry it out a little.

1. To make the colour, you will need purchased pre-coloured black or red fondant, the same amount of white fondant and possibly some colouring paste. We find pre-coloured icing unmanageable on its own, as it

a

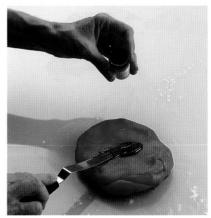

b

is too soft and has too much pigment, therefore we dilute it with white fondant.

2. Start by mixing pre-coloured red or black icing and white fondant icing in a 50/50 ratio (Pic a). To get the intense colour you desire, you may also need to add some colour paste (Pic b). Do this after you have mixed the icing and gradually top up the colour until you reach the desired intensity, kneading it in well (Pic c).

c

MARBLING

Marbling is a simple technique that creates an effective swirled pattern in the fondant.

1. Start with two small portions of fondant icing in different colours of your choice. Roll each portion of fondant into a rope and then twist them together (Pic a).

2. Roll the twisted rope into a ball in the palm of your hands (Pic b). Take care not to over-knead it. or the colours will fuse into a single shade.

3. Flatten the ball slightly. Sprinkle your work surface with a little cornflour and roll out the fondant to the desired thickness (Pic c).

4. Cut out shapes and use as desired (Pic d).

a

b

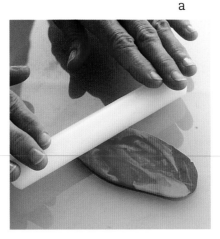

c

d

EDIBLE GLITTER

Non-toxic edible glitter is available from cake decorating supply stores and is easy to apply.

1. Trace over the area where you wish to apply the glitter with a paintbrush coated with water, piping gel or syrup (Pic a).

2. Dust the wet area with edible glitter and wait until dry (Pic b).

3. Dust away the excess glitter with a perfectly dry, soft brush (Pic c).

a

c

c

EDIBLE PAINTING

Use colour pastes, cake decorating alcohol and fine or medium paintbrushes for painting. Dilute a small amount of colour paste with alcohol to the desired consistency. Test the paint on a piece of icing first and keep adding either colour paste or alcohol until you get the intensity of colour you want. We recommend painting on white or light-coloured icing (Pic a).

BLUSH

To create rosy cheeks, mix red and pink petal dust to the desired colour in a small container, then use a dry fine paintbrush to rub it in (Pic b). Use this paintbrush only for applying blush, as the rubbing will divide the bristles and the brush will no longer be suitable for fine painting work. Alternatively, you can use a small make-up brush.

PAINTING IN SILVER/GOLD

For this technique, you will need edible silver or gold lustre dust, which can be found in nearly all cake decorating supply stores.

Mix the dust with cake decorating alcohol and then, using a fine paintbrush, apply it to the icing (Pic c).

As they are very fine, silver and gold dust can spread everywhere and contaminate your cakes and decorations. Be sure to place paper underneath your project when using the dust and, if you are painting directly onto the cake itself, try to cover unpainted areas of the cake with paper before proceeding.

a

b

c

EYES

Well-executed eyes can make your cupcakes look professional—as well as adding character to each face. It's not difficult to paint life-like eyes: choose the appropriate technique and follow the simple steps. Piping gel is an important part of each technique; it keeps the eyes bright and shiny. **Note:** This is a more advanced method than the one used in the projects in this book.

Eye 1
Roll a small ball of black icing and flatten slightly. Paint with piping gel. When dry, add a dot of white-white colour paste for highlight (Pic a).

Eye 2
Roll a small ball of chosen eye colour and flatten slightly. Paint with piping gel. Paint black pupil and apply more gel. Paint white-white highlight dot (Pic b).

Eye 3
Roll a small ball of black icing and flatten slightly. Paint with piping gel. Use white-white colour paste to paint two highlight dots, one larger than the other (Pic c).

Eye 4
Roll a small ball of white icing and flatten slightly. Paint the iris with your chosen colour. Paint black pupil and outline the iris with black. When dry, paint with piping gel. Paint white-white highlight (Pic d).

a

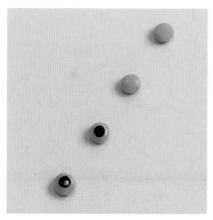

b

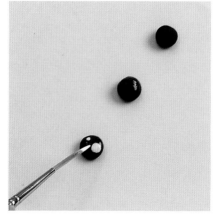

c

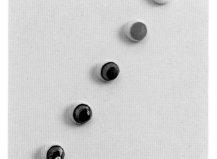

d

MAKING A TEMPLATE

Making templates is an essential part of cake decorating, allowing you to cut any shape. Choose a reference, such as a font or picture. You may need to photocopy the design to either enlarge or reduce it to the desired size to suit your cupcake. Once you have a reference, there are two basic ways to make a template.

Method A

Using a fine-tip pen and either a round template or a round cutter the same size as your cupcake icing, trace a circle (or circles) onto your artwork, so that the design is in the centre of the circle. Cover the artwork with a piece of tracing paper. Using either your hand or tape to hold the tracing paper steady, trace over the image and the circle outline, using a fine-tip pen.

Turn the tracing paper over (to get the mirror image) and carefully trace over the previously traced design lines with a soft 2B pencil. You do not need to trace over the circles—they are a placement guide only.

Method B

For this method you will need a lightbox, but you can improvise by using a sunny window or even a lamp under a glass-topped coffee table.

On top of the lightbox, flip your reference artwork over onto the wrong side. If you are using a window, tape the image, right side down, to the window. Because of the light source, you will be able to see the outline clearly in mirror image. Place the tracing paper over the reversed image and, using a pen, trace the circles to define the cupcake outlines. Then, using a 2B pencil, trace the design inside the circles onto the tracing paper.

TRANSFERRING A TEMPLATE

Once you have made a template for your chosen design, you need to transfer the outline onto the icing, so you can cut it out or use it as a guide for placing decorations on the cupcake.

Place the tracing on the icing, with the mirror-image 2B pencil lines face-down on the icing itself. If the icing is soft, a light sweep across the paper with your hand is often enough to transfer the pencil outline onto the icing. If the icing is harder, trace or rub over the lines on the tracing paper with a skewer at a 45-degree angle, taking care not to dent the icing with too much pressure.

You can now use a small sharp knife to cut accurately along the transferred lines or use them as a guide to place cut-out decorations.

Tip
- If you plan to use your templates repeatedly, you can make them more permanent by tracing the outlines onto waxy cardboard and cutting them out. By keeping your templates and template boards, you can amass a library and save time in the future.

TEMPLATES

Cheeky Monkey

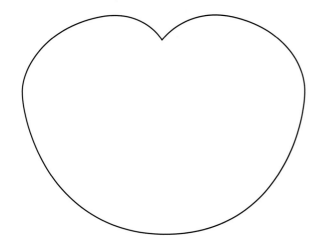

Freddy

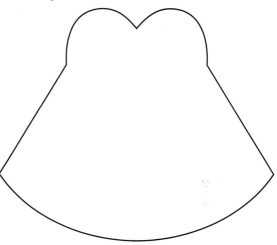

Cupcake

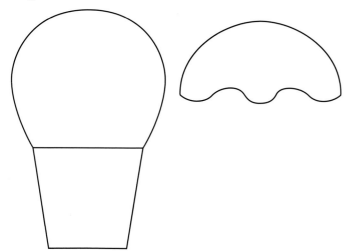

Hairy Foot

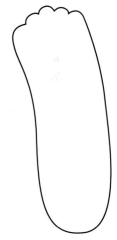

Double Happiness

Troubleshooting

DRY ICING

If your icing is dry and cracking it will be almost impossible to work with. Cracking can be the result of a number of different causes. You might be over-kneading the icing and drying it out; or the environment (air conditioning or an over-heated room) could be a factor; perhaps you are taking too long to work with the icing—you must work quickly; or you may have used too much Tylose powder. Whatever the cause, to remedy the problem, brush a little water on the icing and then knead it through. Alternatively, you can brush in a small amount of glycerine and knead it through. If you are constantly suffering from dry icing, you might need to change the fondant brand you use or address the environment, such as air conditioning or heating, both of which will dry icing out.

HUMIDITY

This is a cake decorator's worst enemy: decorations don't adhere, icing becomes soft and sticky and it's almost impossible to use. At Planet Cake, we mix sifted icing sugar into the icing a little at a time and knead it through. Another method is to mix Tylose powder into the icing.

STAINS

If your icing is stained with cornflour, use cake decorating alcohol applied with a soft paintbrush to remove the cornflour stains; pat dry with a tissue. If your icing is stained with chocolate, you will need to employ a more complex method. First, using a soft paintbrush, wash the stain lightly with warm, soapy water, then rinse the brush and gently wash the soap away with clean water. Pat lightly dry with a tissue and then lightly dust with cornflour using a soft brush.

PAPER CASES PEELING

When the paper cases peel away from the sides of the cupcake, this is usually the result of humidity and is sometimes caused when they are covered with icing too quickly before being given enough time to cool.

The icing traps the heat in the cupcake and the humidity makes the paper peel. There is nothing you can do about this, so remember to always allow enough cooling time for your cupcakes.

WET ICING

Wet icing is usually the result of too much colour pigment and often black, red and brown icing become 'wet' and difficult to work with. The remedy is the same as for humidity: knead sifted icing sugar into the icing.

CUPCAKES COOKING UNEVENLY

This is probably a result of your oven not cooking at an even temperature. All ovens are different; they can also have hot and cold spots. For example, cupcakes at the back of the oven may not bake as well as those at the front. We recommend baking a maximum of 24 cupcakes in the oven at any one time. If you need to move the cupcakes around to compensate for hot/cold spots, wait 15 minutes after first putting them in before opening the door again to move them.

CUPCAKES SINKING

Do not disturb your cupcakes in the first 15 minutes of baking; this is their period to become structurally sound. If you open the oven door in the first 15 minutes, or take the cupcakes out of the oven prematurely, they may sink.

CUPCAKES TOO FULL

Only fill the paper cases two-thirds full with mix to avoid spilling and cupcake collapse. If this has happened, you can, however, trim off the worst of the excess before covering with ganache.

CUPCAKES CRACKING

Cupcakes can crack because the oven is too hot: the mixture is being cooked too quickly and it is being forced out the top like lava instead of baking evenly. Reduce the temperature of the oven by 10°C (50°F) and see if this makes a difference.

SWEATY CUPCAKES

Shiny sweaty cupcakes are the result of keeping the cupcakes in a closed container; even a closed cake box can make them sweat and the icing will become shiny and sticky. Be sure to store your cupcakes with the lid off until they need to travel, but keep a cloth over the top to prevent colour fading.

GANACHE SEPARATING

Ganache separates when the cream is not mixed with the chocolate immediately: leaving the cream on top of the chocolate without emulsifying will cause the chocolate to separate. If this happens, whisk the mixture vigorously, put it in the fridge for 10 minutes to cool a little, then stir with a whisk again.

LUMPY GANACHE

If your ganache is lumpy, it is perhaps because you have not mixed the chocolate with the cream thoroughly or the chocolate hasn't completely melted. Give it another good stir and if this doesn't work reheat it over a saucepan of simmering water or with short bursts in the microwave until the chocolate melts. Stir well.

Glossary

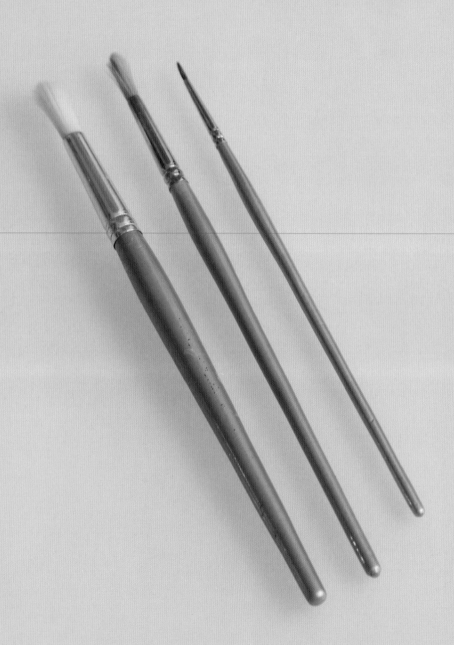

CAKE DECORATING ALCOHOL
This contains 5 per cent rose essence and is used to mix with colour paste or colour liquid for painting. It is also used for removing icing stains. Vodka can be used as a substitute.

CORNFLOUR
Also known as cornstarch, cornflour is the starch of the maize grain. It is used in cake decorating for dusting work surfaces when rolling out the icing. It is better to use than icing sugar when rolling icing. Use sparingly as it can dry the icing out.

COUVERTURE
Couverture is a natural, sweet chocolate containing no added fats other than cocoa butter. It is used for dipping, moulding, coating and, most importantly, for ganache making. Not to be confused with confectionery chocolate or compound chocolate, couverture is a very high-quality chocolate that contains extra cocoa butter and is usually sold in the form of buttons. The higher percentage of cocoa butter, combined with the processing, gives the

chocolate more sheen, a firmer 'snap' when broken, and a creamy mellow flavour. We use a couverture chocolate with about 44–63 per cent cocoa content. This is a mid-range couverture chocolate, a little superior to what you would normally find in a supermarket. It is available from cake decorating supply stores or speciality cooking stores, although you can sometimes find it in large supermarkets.

CUTTERS

Available in different sizes and shapes—such as rounds, flowers and hearts—cutters often come in sets, in plastic or stainless steel. For covering cupcakes, you need a round cutter that is the same size as the top of the cupcakes, as well as one that is one size larger; a full set of round cutters is invaluable.

EDIBLE GLITTER

Available in an array of colours from cake decorating supply stores. Apply edible glitter with water or piping gel.

FLEXI-SMOOTHER

A flexi-smoother is a Planet Cake DIY invention. We use either unused X-ray film (which can be hard to get) or a thin plastic, such as acetate, computer film or the plastic used for flexible display folders (the ones with the plastic sleeves inside). Cut the plastic to a rectangle, a little larger than the palm of your hand. Round the edges using scissors, then disinfect the plastic and hey presto!

Use the flexi-smoother to buff and polish the icing, helping you create razor-sharp edges and very smooth surfaces. The flexi-smoother is flexible so you can manipulate it with your hand to navigate the icing of shaped and complex cakes to eliminate all the air bubbles and bumps in the icing, resulting in a smooth, perfect and professional-looking icing finish.

FONDANT ICING

Fondant is a dough-like icing that can be rolled out, then cut out to cover cakes. It is used to cover both large cakes and cupcakes. In its ready-made form, it is also called RTR (ready-to-roll), plastic icing and sugar paste. The basic ingredient of fondant is icing sugar, with the addition of gelatine, liquid glucose and glycerine to provide a malleable, sweet paste. Most ready-made fondant comes in white or ivory and can be tinted to any colour of the rainbow.

Fondant gives cakes a beautiful, porcelain-like surface that can be painted, piped onto, cut out or stamped—the possibilities are virtually endless. Fondant is also used to 'model' and cut 3D shapes for decoration. Good-quality ready-made fondant is costly, but worth the investment. You will need to experiment with different brands to find the one that suits your needs. It is available from large supermarkets and cake decorating supply stores.

FOOD OR ICING COLOURS

Colour paste is the most concentrated of food colours. Mix it into fondant icing or thin it with cake decorating alcohol to paint with. Liquid colouring is similar, but less intense.

FRILLING TOOL

Part of a set called 'modelling tools', this tool is named because it is used to 'frill' soft surfaces, but it is probably the most versatile tool in the box, and is the one we use on almost every cake in this book—to score lines, indent facial features, mark textured surfaces for fur and hair, and so on.

GANACHE

In its simplest form, ganache is equal parts chocolate and cream. Ganache can be made with dark, milk or white chocolate, or with a combination of all three. We use it to give a smooth and even surface to a cupcake before covering it with fondant icing.

GLUE

To fix decorations or sections of icing to the top of cupcakes, simply add a dab of water. Use this 'adhesive' to attach the components as you would use glue, taking care not to get things too wet. You can also use syrup or piping gel for extra hold.

PAINTING

Mix edible colour paste or liquid colour with cake decorating alcohol, then paint onto fondant-covered cakes with a fine artist's brush.

PALETTE KNIFE

Usually a handled flat knife with a bend (crank) in the blade, often called cranked palette knife. It is used to spread and smooth ganache onto cakes and cupcakes.

PASTA MACHINE

Also called a pasta maker, it is used, as the name suggests, for making homemade pasta, but it's also brilliant for rolling out icing, as it provides a consistent thickness and rolls the icing perfectly.

PIPING GEL

Also known as piping jelly, this clear, sticky gel becomes fluid when warmed. It maintains a shiny wet look when set, so is used to give a shine to eyes, tongues and 'liquids'. It can be coloured with colour paste. It is also used for attaching icing decorations.

PIPING TIPS AND COUPLER

The size and shape of the opening on a piping tip determines the type of decoration a tip will produce, although with royal icing, we almost always use the round tips (and very occasionally, a star tip). Round piping tips are used to make dots and outlines, as well as writing and figure piping.

The coupler sits between a material piping bag and piping tip. You can then screw the piping tip onto the coupler and easily change between different sizes and shapes without changing the piping bag.

PETAL AND LUSTRE DUSTS

These dusts can be mixed with cake decorating alcohol to give a metallic lustre to decorations. Red and/or pink petal dust can be brushed on dry to give cheeks a rosy glow.

PRE-COLOURED ICING

To make red or black icing, you will need pre-coloured icing, available from cake decorating supply stores. The advantage of pre-coloured icing is the intensity of the colour pigment.

ROLLING PINS

A small rolling pin is ideal for small projects and rolling out small pieces of icing. You can buy a fancy one from a cake decorating supply store, but the most prized small rolling pins at Planet Cake are those found in children's baking sets.

We also use large rolling pins to roll out icing. The types available are: without handles, with integral handles or, our favourite, with handles that are attached to a central rod in the roller. Rolling pins, whether made from wood, marble or silicon, should have absolutely smooth surfaces, with no dints or marks that will transfer to your icing.

ROYAL ICING

A mixture of egg white (or albumen) and icing sugar with a little lemon juice or vinegar, royal icing is used for piping decorations onto cupcakes. It dries hard and can be coloured with edible food colour. You can buy instant royal icing powder where you just have to add water, or you can make your own.

SYRUP OR SOAKING SYRUP

A mixture of boiled water and jam in the ratio of 1:1; used to moisten surfaces of cut cakes or between the ganache and icing covering to help adhere the icing. It can be flavoured with alcohol.

TYLOSE POWDER

If mixed into rolled fondant, marzipan or royal icing, this non-toxic chemical—carboxymethylcellulose (CMC)—forms a strong modelling paste that dries hard. Tylose powder can also be mixed with water to make thick, strong edible glue.

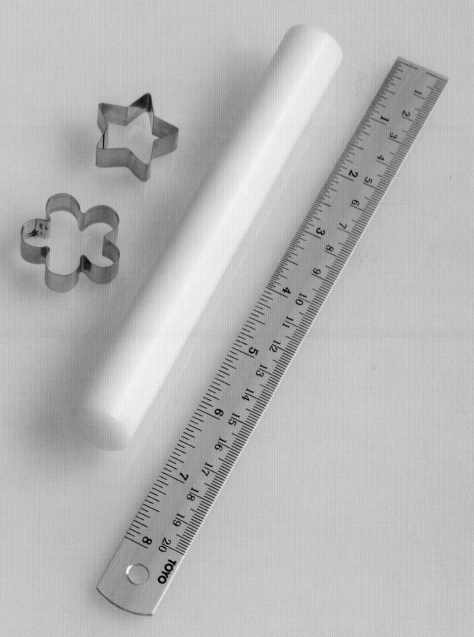

Index

Acknowledgments

Firstly I need to thank my first charity partner, Oz Harvest, and everyone who has assisted me in hosting the Christmas Charity Cupcake Drive events, particularly my wonderful Planet Cake staff. These crazy cupcake drives planted the seed from which many cake events and, indeed, this very book started, and still give me so much joy to host. In addition, I would like to thank the volunteers and guests that have come to all our cake events; we cannot have a party without you guys, thanks for coming!

I am very grateful to the wonderful team at Murdoch Books for yet another wonderful collaboration. Particular thanks to Chris Rennie for taking a leap of faith, and to Kylie Walker, my publisher, for her talents. A huge thanks again to Sarah O'Brien for her incredible style, and Natasha Milne for making my cakes look beautiful. I would also like to thank Emma Samia and Cat Domican, the busiest bees in my business for being consistently professional and always supporting me. A big thank you to my employee and dearest friend Antony Bullimore for the gifts he brings to me and all of Planet Cake; he is a rare and wonderful bird and deserves my deepest gratitude.

Thank you to the Roche family; Anna Maria has always been my rock and sounding board and has again brought her cake decorating talents to one of my books. I feel very blessed to have worked with her for many years and on this book together. It is a joy to work with someone whom I know so well and, as a result, we collaborated effortlessly. I would also like to thank her very talented son, Talin Roche, for his 'Cubie' designs which feature in this book, and a big thank you to Joseph and Kiran for their never ending support and loyalty.

Finally I would like to thank my Mum and Dad for showing me the joy of hosting a great event and enjoying life! I would like to thank my brother Milo and my dearest friends James, Melita and Melanie who honed my party planning experience and inspired many of these projects. Thank you to my delightful daughter, Estelle, who was a guinea pig for many projects in this book and will always be my proudest and most joyful achievement. I would like to specially thank Jono who lent me a musical ear to make cakes with and was indispensible for my most successful event to date, the World's Largest Opera House Cake.

Finally, a whopping big thank you to the Adams family, Cutler family, Lester family, Murray family, Smith and Jones families, Drysdale Communications family and, of course, my precious Planet Cake family—from my heart to yours, thank you!

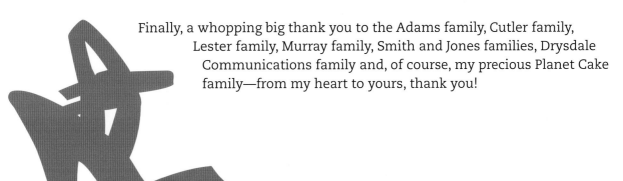

Published in 2011 by Murdoch Books Pty Limited

Murdoch Books Australia
Pier 8/9
23 Hickson Road
Millers Point NSW 2000
Phone: +61 (0) 2 8220 2000
Fax: +61 (0) 2 8220 2558
www.murdochbooks.com.au
info@murdochbooks.com.au

Murdoch Books UK Limited
Erico House, 6th Floor
93–99 Upper Richmond Road
Putney, London SW15 2TG
Phone: +44 (0) 20 8785 5995
Fax: +44 (0) 20 8785 5985
www.murdochbooks.co.uk
info@murdochbooks.co.uk

For Corporate Orders & Custom Publishing contact Noel Hammond,
National Business Development Manager

Publisher: Kylie Walker
Designer: Kristine Lindbjerg
Design Coordinator: Tania Gomes
Photographer: Natasha Milne
Stylist: Sarah O'Brien
Project Editor: Gabriella Sterio
Editor: Carol Jacobson
Production: Renee Melbourne

National Library of Australia Cataloguing-in-Publication Data
Author: Cutler, Paris
Title: Planet Cake Celebrate: cake making for all occasions / Paris Cutler
ISBN: 9781742665856 (pbk.)
Notes: Includes index.
Subjects: Cake. Cake decorating. Icings, Cake.
Dewey Number: 641.86539
A catalogue record for this book is available from the British Library.

PRINTED in 2011 by 1010 Printing International Limited, China.

IMPORTANT: Those who might be at risk from the effects of salmonella poisoning (the elderly,
pregnant women, young children and those suffering from immune deficiency diseases) should
consult their doctor with any concerns about eating raw eggs.

OVEN GUIDE: You may find cooking times vary depending on the oven you are using. For fan-forced
ovens, as a general rule, set the oven temperature to 20°C (35°F) lower than indicated in the recipe.